What others say about the "Rediscover the Joy of Learning" Processes

The learning strategies and processes of "Rediscover the Joy of Learning" are being used in four different ways:

1. Individual students, teachers and parents use the book or audio tapes as a study guide in HOW to do academic tasks.

2. Schools bring Dr. Blackerby or Certified Practitioners of the "Joy" processes into their schools for "Staff Development Workshops" based on Joy.

3. Students are coached one-on-one or in small groups in Blackerby's Academic Skills by Dr. Blackerby or a Certified Practitioner of the "Joy" processes.

4. Adult students, teachers, counselors, and parents take the "Rediscover the Joy of Learning" Certification Training so they can help other struggling students.

The following comments come from those who have used the "Joy" processes:

"This book is an exceptionally useful resource for teachers, parents, and anyone who works with students. Don has a gift for writing in a way that makes it easy to understand and apply. The learning and memory strategies alone are worth the price of the book, and the section on motivation is excellent. I recommend it highly."
Charles Dorman, School Psychologist, Iowa, USA

"The year preceding Dr. Don Blackerby's visits to our school, we were listed as a "low performing" school by the State Department of Education. As a result of the staff's work, our students made significant gains by the next year. Our plan was so effective and positive that we continue to use it with a great deal of confidence. Dr. Blackerby's contributions to this plan were significant and greatly appreciated. I was personally very impressed with the practical implications of the Joy processes introduced by Dr. Blackerby in that they not only appreciably improved test scores, they also provided teachers an interesting, dynamic way of teaching subjects which all too often are dull and unexciting. With Dr. Blackerby's learning strategies, once a child has demonstrated that he/she has learned a spelling word, word definition, math fact, etc., the teacher can expect that the learning has been internalized and will be retained with minimal review. For an educator who spends substantial amounts of time re-teaching material already presented, this fact alone makes the use of the Joy processes worthwhile."
Ronda Fleming, Elementary School Principal, Oklahoma, USA

"I am so glad I found you. It took me five months to "hunt" the best possible support for my son (who had been diagnosed ADD) and I know it was worthwhile to bring him to see you. So far he is doing great. I learned a lot, not only to better help my son but also for myself. I'll inform a broad group of therapists/docs/and educators in a chat room (focused on ADD among other things) about our experience with you. I want to do this because I am convinced that your methods are really superior compared to drugs for ADD."
Simone Silvestri, M.D., Ph.D. and Parent, Michigan, USA

"All who knew of my trip have been asking about the course, and about what I thought of it. They are enthusiastic and excited when I tell them of the course and all that I learned and experienced. My Mom wanted to know why she wasn't taught these things when she was in school! I expected to learn how to help my son overcome difficulties he is experiencing in school. I also expected to learn how to help other kids who are struggling, I want to make that my niche in counseling.

I learned very well how to assist him and how to work with kids. I learned "how to learn" in a way which I never knew before. I developed a confidence that I had not had before and know that I can apply all that I learned. I really learned how to use the "Logical Levels," which I knew about but never applied like this. I developed friendships with people from around the world and share our love and support for each other even though we are not in physical contact with each other."
Charmaine Tucker, Nurse and Parent, Canada

"We came to the Joy training with a vision of helping students learn how to learn, and we left with simple and effective ways to implement that vision, and in the very process were ourselves transformed."
Charlotte Saji, LCPC (School Counselor and Academic Coach), Sharon McCarthy (Educational Consultant/Coach), John Pesek, PhD (Statistician and College Teacher), John Franklin Mitchell (Performance and Academic Coach), USA

"Although I have been consistently a top student, I have never felt confident whenever math, of any kind, was involved. Over the years, I have asked a number of teachers for assistance. I was usually told not to worry, I'd do OK because I worked hard. I never felt heard or understood with regards to this issue. I almost didn't pursue an MBA because I knew that math courses were part of the requirements. I decided to go ahead with the MBA and do my best. Although I received A's in my other courses, any course with math was very difficult. I hired a tutor to help. At the end of my MBA course work, I took the comprehensive exam and failed the financial portion of it. Nothing on the test looked familiar to me, even though I had spent 95% of my time studying financial information. I decided to visit with Don Blackerby about my math difficulties. Don listened to my comments, then said, "I think this may be happening..." and proceeded to list a sequence of mental events that described exactly what I was experiencing. For the first time in my life, I knew I was talking to someone who understood what I was going through. After meeting with Don one time, I applied the studying techniques in preparation for my economics final. The test seemed easy and I ended up with an A. The professor told me that I had received the highest score on the test."
Rita Crockett, Graduate Student, Oklahoma, USA

"Anyone interested in learning and helping others, especially children—then this Joy training is a must. Opened the windows of my mind and exploded the frontiers of my understanding."
Carole Kinsey, Counselor and NLP Trainer, United Kingdom

For more information: Phone: 1-405-773-8820, e-mail: info@nlpok.com, Web Site: www.nlpok.com

Rediscover The Joy of Learning

Don A. Blackerby, Ph.D.

SUCCESS SKILLS, Inc.
Oklahoma City, Oklahoma

Library of Congress Catalog Card Number: 96-93085

ISBN 1-889997-00-5

Certification to use BLACKERBY'S ACADEMIC SUCCESS SKILLS is available through workshops. Please contact Don Blackerby at SUCCESS SKILLS, Inc. if you are interested.

Don A. Blackerby, Ph.D.
SUCCESS SKILLS, Inc
PO Box 42631
Oklahoma City, OK 73123
(405) 773-8820
1-800-775-3397 USA
Fax (405) 773-5427
info@nlpok.com
Web Site: www.nlpok.com

CONTENTS

FOREWORD

We are sure that you will be amply rewarded for the time you spend reading this book. It offers a wealth of practical, effective processes to Attention Deficit Disorder (ADD) issues. The methods work consistently to help people with learning problems -- they make learning more fun, more satisfying, and easier. Until recently, medication has seemed to be the most helpful approach. While medication has helped some people and provided for classroom and personal management, it has at best only provided a partial answer. The information and processes in this book provide another set of pathways to learning and enjoying learning.

Drawing on his Neuro-Linguistic Programming (NLP) background, Don Blackerby offers a much needed handbook for students, teachers, parents, and counselors. It is a book that will also benefit people who have been diagnosed as having ADD.

Don Blackerby is a former math teacher and college dean who currently offers consulting and training on educational issues through his firm, Success Skills, Inc. His mission is to assist those persons who have challenges in learning in traditional settings. He readily shares how he himself struggled intensely all the way through school, well into his college years, and as a result developed an attitude toward school that kept him from becoming a successful student.

He still remembers a conversation with a friend, a straight A student, that turned this attitude around. From this personal experience came not only a new attitude towards learning, but a passion to discover what it was that had worked to create this shift. He has devoted his career to researching ways to close the gap between what is happening with students in the education system and what he knows is possible. He has been motivated to find an effective yet practical way of working with students who have learning problems similar to those he experienced.

About 20 years ago, Don discovered NLP, a field that was created by modeling the thinking of effective people. He began applying what he was learning about thinking strategies to work with his son who went from an average student to an outstanding honors student using the powerful NLP processes. In his work with students, Don is always aware of the difference between the thinking strategies a student is using when he/she is getting good results versus the strategies he/she is using when stuck.

Throughout the years Don has been systematically applying the strategies already available in NLP while developing new strategies of his own to apply to learning issues. He became committed to writing a handbook on learning while involved in the NLP World Health Community for the 21st Century, a group dedicated to using NLP to heal individuals and systems. Now, this book is the culmination of all of his research.

The unique approaches in this book are presented in three sections. Section 1 shares the specific strategies for learning academic tasks. Section 2 includes communication and motivational techniques helpful to parents, teacher, and counselors in working with students. Section 3 is geared towards the specific learning disabilities labeled Attention Deficit Disorder. Don shares his own refreshing ideas in each section.

Don noticed early on in pursuing his mission that the education system pre-supposes that students naturally know how to learn in the classroom. While it is true that as children we are natural learners, we all can't necessarily transfer these skills to the classroom. One of the goals of the book is to change that situation, so that learning becomes natural even in the classroom setting.

Don demonstrates how powerful NLP modeling can be when applied to a specific area with an outcome in mind. We are inspired by watching Don Blackerby pursue his purpose -- his passion and enthusiasm are like a breath of fresh air. His dedication to the cause is apparent. May you also catch the spirit of enthusiasm with which this book was written.

Suzi Smith and Tim Hallbom
NLP Trainers/Authors
Co-founders of Western States Training Associates and
Anchor Point Associates

PREFACE

This book has been written in two styles. The part covering academic skills is in a "cookbook" -- step 1, step 2, step 3 -- fashion. I figured you may not want to read any theory or background information or anecdotes -- you just want to KNOW WHAT TO DO. The other parts give more reasons why certain procedures are done and also some stories or anecdotes to help liven up and explain the information.

The writing of this book has changed my life. I now am traveling all over the world leading workshops on the contents of the book to teachers, counselors and parents of struggling students. More and more, I go into schools and directly teach the struggling students. In fact, some of my most recent research (and probably my next book) is about the "troubled" (or "at risk" or "high challenge") youth of our society, how they got there and, more importantly, what we as parents and teachers can do for them. Also, my 14 day certification workshop, "Rediscover the Joy of Learning," is sending highly qualified and inspired individuals out around the world--and they are **TRANSFORMING STUDENTS' LIVES**. I am truly blessed.

Most of the expertise which allows me to do the things covered in this handbook comes from the field of Neuro-Linguistic Programming (NLP) (See Appendix A). These learning strategies and techniques, therefore, are the results of NLP being applied to the learning process. Non-NLP trained individuals, therefore, should be able to utilize these techniques. The only exception might be in the section dealing with Attention Deficit Disorder (ADD). In order to do some of the prescribed techniques, a certified practitioner of NLP should be consulted.

I have learned from so many people that it is impossible to thank them all. Besides my students and clients, who I always learn from, some of the NLP trainers who contributed to my journey are: John Grinder, Judith DeLozier, Richard Bandler, Robert Dilts, Tim Hallbom, Suzi Smith, Leslie Cameron-Bandler, and Steve and Connirae Andreas. Thanks to all of them for putting up with all my questions.

Enjoy. I expect to receive feedback as to how you have used it and how I can improve my next edition.

Don A. Blackerby, Ph.D.
Oklahoma City, Oklahoma, April, 1999

INTRODUCTION

The United States is the land of opportunity. Our children have the opportunity to participate in public educational programs designed to prepare them for academic and personal excellence in their future endeavors. Recent reports reveal that the public educational system may be less than successful in achieving this goal. Results of the 1993 National Adult Literacy Survey indicate that approximately 50% of the adults in this country do not possess the reading and computational skills necessary to excel in today's modern technological society. Perhaps the more appalling aspect of this study is that 90% of these adults report they believe that their skill level in these areas are either "good" or "excellent". They do not realize that they don't know.

A significant number of these low skilled adults are unemployed, receive public assistance, or reside in our nation's correctional facilities. The Center for Study of Literacy at Northeastern State University in Oklahoma has been evaluating educational levels and programs at correctional facilities in the State of Oklahoma since 1991. These evaluations indicate that 48% of Oklahoma's offenders read below the 9th grade level and approximately 80% of these offenders have been diagnosed as learning disabled at some time in their public educational career. These figures are similar to results of studies in other states. It is apparent that opportunities for students who do not succeed in our public educational system are limited and society as well as the individual student pays an exorbitant price.

The learning strategies and techniques Dr. Blackerby covers in *Rediscover the Joy of Learning* **will** make a significant difference in an individual student's achievement when used at school, home, or any learning situation. These techniques teach a student how to learn, not just what to learn. Our public schools presuppose that a student already knows how to learn and focuses on content rather than the process of learning. Knowing how to learn is not only necessary for academic success, it is vital for success in our rapidly changing society.

We have been privileged to have trained and worked with Dr. Blackerby for several years. We have seen many young people, who have struggled in the educational system, excel using Dr. Blackerby's learning techniques. These students range from "bright but bored" learners to those students who have been labeled and served in Special Education Programs.

This handbook is written in a very "user-friendly" style and can be used by non-professional as well as professional educators. The techniques and strategies detailed in this book will benefit students, parents, teachers, and all those interested in rediscovering the joy of learning and achieving academic and personal excellence.

P. Frank McKane, Ph.D., Director
Center for Study of Literacy
Oklahoma Literacy Clearinghouse
Northeastern State University
Tahlequah, Oklahoma

Margaret R. McKane, M.Ed.
Certifications; LD, MR, SED
Tahlequah Public Schools
Tahlequah, Oklahoma

BACKGROUND

The Problem

Since the report "A Nation At Risk" came out in 1983 contending that there are inadequacies in our educational system, there have been many other reports and studies screaming for public officials to solve the problems. The proposed solutions have been varied and numerous.

For many students in today's educational system, school is a price to pay to be with friends. For them, school is some place to go because their parents and society say they must. Some of these students are pretty good at the academics while others suffer through the time spent in the classroom in great agony, hoping against hope that somehow a miracle will occur and they will scrape through. Others rebel, refusing to go to class and, eventually, they drop out.

> ### For many students...school is a price to pay to be with friends.

For the students who stay, many sit for long periods of time staring at textbooks, going over and over the written material and realizing that not much is being retained -- *frustrated and bored and not knowing what to do differently.* Many study for hours and then when test time comes they "blank out" and can't remember what they thought they had learned -- *frustrated and bored not knowing what to do differently.* Many sit through countless hours of class lecture, not having any idea what the teacher is talking about or of the importance of the material to them -- *frustrated and bored not knowing what to do differently.*

It's no wonder that so many of these students have bought into the non-learner labels that schools and society have assigned to them, especially when they compare their actions and performance on the sports field and in their hobbies with their actions and performance in the classroom.

In sports and in their hobbies, they learn or are coached in **HOW** to do the skills necessary to achieve the desired outcome. In the classroom, it is often "assumed" they know the "academic skills"; how to learn, how to read, how to read with comprehension, how to memorize, how to listen, and how to stay interested. And, if they don't know these things, something must be wrong with them. But when were they coached in academic skills? And, shouldn't they have been?

Most students do what they think will work. If it doesn't work well, the diligent students will try harder (usually over long periods of time) until they are frustrated and fall behind the other students -- resulting in emotional problems, behavior problems, and loss of self-esteem.

Students face pressure to do better without the necessary instructions on HOW to improve or WHAT to do differently.

This phenomenon is happening to a large number of our students. We call them "the underachievers." Some other labels they are sometimes given are; stupid, learning disabled, rebellious, and apathetic. What they are also given is a lot of pressure from family, teachers, peers and society to do better. Pressure to do better without the necessary instructions on **HOW** to improve or **WHAT** to do differently.

In one sense, some are lucky when they find something to turn to in which they can succeed -- an activity, hobby, sport, or gang. This helps preserve the student's self-esteem. Other students do not find such an opportunity and they lose self-esteem and drop out, and/or turn to drugs, and/or have behavior problems.

When students find alternative activities in which they can succeed (such as sports, scouting, cars, or skate boarding, for example) it is an easy choice to concentrate on the alternative and to spend more time on it and less time on academics. When this happens, they tend to get further and further behind in academics. And, as they get further behind yet higher on the academic ladder, the courses get harder and the academic skills which are needed get more sophisticated, the inevitable happens and they give up in frustration.

What is needed are new reading and learning strategies and skills which will fit the more sophisticated material they are learning. Strategies which will enable students to succeed in school by making the appropriate logical connections for learning to occur.

The normal types of study skills (while they may be helpful in some isolated cases) have proven over and over again **NOT** to be the skills that will make the difference in the underachiever. The types of skills that will make the difference are at a more basic logical level. They are grounded more in the process of HOW knowledge, information and comprehension is stored in the mind, and in HOW interest in learning and school is engaged and maintained.

> The reason the students don't know the skills to learn in the classroom is that we (society and school systems) presupposed that students naturally knew how to learn in the classroom **AND** that they knew how to learn very well. This is an erroneous presupposition.

I have many parents call about their child's attitude or behavior in school. Their prevailing cry over and over again is "My child used to enjoy school so much and now they don't want to go and are doing poorly in their schoolwork!" When I ask when this shift occurred, the answer is consistently "Around the 5th grade!." Most parents (and students) are totally frustrated and don't know what to do.

In my research, I noted that at about the 5th grade level, a major shift occurs in the academic experience of many students. It appears that the learning and reading strategy most students had used in the earlier grades quits working. Many students, to their credit, keep trying to make it work, but it usually doesn't help.

**Why does this occur around the 5th grade?
I don't know for sure, but I have a theory.**

Most students learn to read by sounding out the words of their reading material and, if they can sound out the words without faltering, they (and others) consider them good readers. Think about it. If you were told to help a child read, what would you do? Most of us would sit with the child and listen to them sound out the words. We would correct the words they would stumble over -- right? If they could sound out all the words without any problem, we would consider the task accomplished.

But is this really reading? In particular, is this reading with any kind of comprehension? Is this kind of reading interesting enough to keep a student focused and attentive? The answer to all of these questions is **NO!**

Without going into a lot of detail, I assess a student's reading strategy in my office by observing him read material with which he is having trouble. I then compare this with how he reads material he enjoys and can learn easily -- it may be a magazine or novel. The student will read the two types of material differently! In every case so far, when students I assess are having trouble, they are simply sounding out the words, and NOTHING ELSE is happening inside their brain. The words figuratively "go in one ear and out the other". When they read the other reading material, they read it visually. That is, they make pictures of the meaning of the material.

So, why the shift at about the 5th grade? My theory is as follows: In the lower grades, the books had a lot of pictures and the material they were reading was usually about common and everyday experiences.   There was, therefore, a synthesia which connected the sound of the word with images, feelings, tastes, and smells of the experience. As the child progresses to about the 5th grade, the pictures in the books decline and the content is more abstract and complex. The child does not have a natural connection between the sound of the word and a sensory experience of the meaning of the word -- AND MOST UNDERACHIEVERS DON'T REALIZE THEY CAN CREATE ONE! The child reads the material and realizes it is not understood and does what he knows to do -- go back and read it again. Some of them read it more s-l-o-w-l-y. This becomes boring, is very ineffective, and the typical child will tire.

Students also find it more interesting and are more successful when they visually learn during the other "academic tasks" that are assigned to them. Tasks such as learning spelling words, math facts, memorizing data, etc., are learned more easily and quickly, if the student will visually learn them. Most of this handbook is about "how" to do that.

This phenomena was discovered by comparing many students' learning strategies when they were successfully learning something to when they were having difficulty. The results were startling and conclusive. When students learn visually they tend to be more interested and learn quickly and easily. When they don't learn visually, they struggle.

The amazing part of this phenomena is that the decision to learn visually or not appears to be random. It can vary by subject matter or teacher or even different material in the same course. It varies randomly because the typical student does not know to strategically learn. That is, the typical student does not know how to decide upon the best way to learn in specific situations. He or she * doesn't know that he is supposed to make this decision because it is presupposed by everybody that he knows how to learn in the classroom and that he knows how to learn well. He doesn't! Learning from books in a classroom is not a natural experience! Children have to be taught to learn in the classroom.

Learning from books in a classroom is not a natural experience! Children have to be taught to learn in the classroom.

Think about students of today and how they were reared. Is the visual field a major part of their life? They have been reared on TV, videos, movies, and computers. The visual field seems to be more interesting to the students of today. And yet they read by sounding out the words and fail to form pictures.

In the following pages, we will explore some of these basic skills for students. The major assumption of this handbook is that most students' problems are caused by missing or inadequate academic skills and, if we learn successful academic skills, many of these problems would no longer exist. The reason the students don't know the skills needed to learn in the classroom is that we (society and school systems) presupposed that students naturally knew how to learn in the classroom **AND** that they knew how to learn very well. This is an erroneous presupposition.

Also in the following pages, we will cover new "learning styles" which have been discovered. Learning styles are preferred ways to learn. It has a lot to do with how information is presented by the teacher or perceived by the student.

---

*Author's note--How do I handle the gender language of she or he? I have decided to alternate sometimes. However, in the interest of having the material flow, I will probably go with one or the other rather than using language such as he or she, him or her, etc.

In some cases, if the material to be learned does not match the student's learning style, she will turn off and not become motivated to learn. In other cases, the learning styles (if the student is not flexible) precludes the student from being successful in certain subjects, or with certain types of teachers, or in certain academic tasks.

When most educators and parents talk about learning styles, they talk about finding the learning style of the student and "teaching to it." This presupposes that any learning style is appropriate for any subject or academic task. I don't think that is correct. If we want students to move toward excellence, we must teach them the best way to learn ALL subjects -- which means they need to learn how to use all learning styles.

When most educators and parents talk about learning styles, they talk about finding the learning style of the student and "teaching to it." This presupposes that any learning style is appropriate for any subject or academic task. I don't think that is correct.

> If we want students to move toward excellence, we must teach them the best way to learn ALL subjects -- which means they need to learn how to use all learning styles.

Another section contains tips for teachers and parents on how to deal with students. These tips are primarily communication tips. Included also are some very important strategies on motivating students and how to affect their attitude. There are also some tips on how to affect self-esteem and limiting beliefs.

The last section is on Learning Disabilities -- primarily Dyslexia and Attention Deficit Disorder (ADD). This section contains some new information and tips on ways to help the students who have been given these labels.

Your Memory And How It Works

Often in school, students are asked to remember some important information. This may be spelling words, vocabulary words, dates, names, etc. Too many times the students flounder around trying very hard to memorize the information and yet when test time comes, they find that they cannot remember it. Many times this comes from the fact that they have no idea how their memory works or how to store and retrieve information in their brain. The following is one way that is useful -- particularly in academic subjects.

In order for your memory to work for you and for you to trust your memory, you need to know the following:

♦   Where you are storing the information.
♦   That you have the information well represented internally.
♦   How to retrieve the information.

Your choices of where to store information are limited to your five senses -- visual, auditory, kinesthetic (touch and feeling), smell, or taste. In school, for all practical purposes, you are limited to auditory, kinesthetic, and/or visual.

The auditory field has a major limitation in that it is linear. That is, you can only consciously process one word at a time and it has to be in a particular order. It is, therefore, very slow. For many students the auditory field is also very boring. The auditory field is very useful in singing, reciting, and other subjects requiring auditory recall. In the academic subjects, it is most useful for retrieval purposes.

The kinesthetic field is very useful in sports, typing, and other like type "use the body" subjects, but for most of the academic subjects it is difficult to store information in and it is also very slow.

While all three play an important part in memory, your visual field has many advantages. It is the fastest. It is the most interesting to students of today who were brought up on TV. You can store vast amounts of information in one picture and access any part of it instantly.

So, for academic subjects like spelling, vocabulary, history, math, etc, the best field to store the information is in the visual field. That is, make internal pictures in your mind's eye of whatever it is you are trying to remember. It may be the actual word or date or it may be a picture of the meaning of the word. Later we will cover how the auditory and kinesthetic fields can be very useful in the third point above -- that is in how to retrieve information.

Now that we know to store the information in pictures, the question arises about the second point-- how to know we have a good picture. The answer is easy but takes practice for some people. If you are trying to store a word, for example, you take a picture of WHAT THE WORD LOOKS LIKE. When you think you have a good clear picture in your mind's eye, you spell the word backwards -- from right to left. This is a check to see if you have a good picture because you can only smoothly spell the word backwards if you have a good picture.

Once you can do this, the question arises about how to retrieve it. Many tests in school are given auditorially -- that is, the teacher asks the question or the student reads the question by sounding out the words. Therefore, we want the sound of the words to "hook" or bring up the picture of the information so the student can answer the question off his or her internal picture.

The fact that you are looking at the picture WHILE saying the information, logically connects the sound and the picture.

This will happen if you connect the sound of the information to the internal picture. To do this, you simultaneously say the information while you hold the picture of the information in your mind's eye. The fact that you are looking at the picture WHILE saying the information, logically connects the sound and the picture. A student learning a spelling word, for example, needs to practice this sound and picture connection about 6 to 8 times, preferably over several days.

Developing a Visual Learning Strategy

One of the most common problems that some students have is the tendency to NOT overlap the words they hear or read into visual images. This creates several problems with these students. First, they have to resort to a slower learning strategy such as auditory or kinesthetic. The visual strategy is significantly faster. Second, for most academic subjects the auditory and kinesthetic strategies are inappropriate and even boring, so the student who does not know how to make these images is forced to work longer and harder at a task that is boring and ineffective. Guess what this student's reaction will be when he is faced with the task of doing his homework or of paying attention in the classroom?

One of the most common problems that some students have is the tendency to NOT overlap the words they hear or read into visual images.

Why would the students not overlap the words they read and hear into visual images? Obviously, to me anyway, most of them don't know they are supposed to do it! I have had students show amazement and surprise at the idea that they could make up their own pictures for the words they were reading off the pages of their textbooks.

One of the causes of this seems to occur in the transition of the reading instruction from the early grades to the middle grades. In the early grades when a word is introduced to the student, a picture of the object is displayed next to the word. The student has a natural bridge from seeing and saying the word to having an internal image of the object. If the instruction also requests the student to access an experience the student has had relative to the object, then the word also has a bridge to the kinesthetic (having the student find a use for the word or make up a sentence using the word can also create a kinesthetic experience for the student).

This practice is fairly quickly discontinued, however, and the students have to make up their own pictures. As students get older and the words get more abstract, it becomes less natural and harder to do and nobody seems to inform them that they should make pictures of the material and some never get around to it.

Because of the way reading is taught in the grade schools, some students learn to read by just saying the words, either externally or internally. They do not overlap into either visual or kinesthetic unless they already have a overlap accidentally installed in their heads by personal experience. For example, a student who has taken a trip to the nation's Capital and personally observed a copy of the Constitution will have a rich visual/auditory/kinesthetic representation of the word Constitution. When he reads that word in a history book, for example, the rich internal representation will be elicited. Obviously, the schools can't rely on all students having these kinds of experiences in all of the subjects they teach.

It seems to me that these rich internal representations can be deliberately internally generated by the students and that the schools need to teach how to do this to those students who have not yet figured it out. In fact, one of the primary differences between the better students and the struggling students is this very ability. The good students either lucked into the technique or learned it on their own and the struggling students just haven't learned how to do it -- yet.

In fact, one of the primary differences between the better students and the struggling students is this very ability.

So, what do the students do who haven't yet learned to do this? Besides not doing their homework, or at least procrastinating on doing it, what kind of learning strategies do they come up with to attempt to do their homework? Well, in my experience some are very ingenious.

I had one very well meaning teenager in my office whose primary complaint was that her studying took her too long, much longer than her fellow students. It seemed to her that what the other students could get accomplished in one hour, took her several hours to do -- and it was getting worse with the passing years. This was a very conscientious student who wanted to succeed in school but was becoming very depressed by her lack of success and the downward trend of her grades. In fact, it was affecting her self-esteem and her attitude about school.

When I elicited her reading strategy, I found that she used a very complicated auditory strategy. After she had read for a while (by sounding out the words internally), she would realize she did not know what she had read and go back and read it again -- this time slower! After trying it a couple of times slower and slower, she would go back to each major word and auditorially insert the definition of the word in the sentence. Guess what that did to her reading speed?

The major words would be words for which she did not have a visual representation. In her case, because her parents had provided a rich background, she had some internal representations of abstract words but not all. She literally would have holes in her comprehension of what she was reading. That's why she would go back and insert definitions of the major words. She would ultimately comprehend, but only after much effort and in a time consuming manner.

Another young man had much the same problem only he had not had the rich experiences the young lady had so he didn't have holes in his comprehension, he just didn't have any comprehension. He was also a dedicated student who spent all of his spare time studying. He was a seventh grade student who quit building his reading vocabulary (visual representation) when the schools quit giving him pictures with words. As the words got more and more abstract, he got further and further behind because all he could do was slow down his reading and try again and again. The only words that elicited a visual representation in him were words that described objects or actions in his real world. This is quite a limitation in school.

The tragedy of both of these students was that both had very good internal visual representation -- they could internally picture things vividly when they were instructed to do so. They simply had never been told that this was a vital link in their reading and learning strategy.

The biggest tragedy of all, however, is the uncountable number of students that were like these two students and never learned these techniques and just checked out of learning and school. They not only are missing out on the joys of learning and of reading for pleasure for all the rest of their life, but many of them suffer self-esteem and attitude problems because they couldn't do what all their peers around them were doing and they couldn't do what society told them was necessary to do to be successful in life.

So what can be done with these students? Can they be taught the visualization skills necessary to become a good student? Can they be turned back on to school and learning? Can the damage to their self-esteem be repaired? Can they be taught to read and learn so that it is interesting? The answer to all these questions is -- YES!! Read on!

Summary

To be able to visualize in rich detail, to be able to hold the image so steady you can copy off it, to be able to instantly access large amounts of information, is a skill so significantly valuable for succeeding in school. The students who do it have an easier time and do far better in school then the students who don't. The students who have not yet learned how to do it get further and further behind as the subjects get more and more complicated. They get more and more frustrated and some real self-image problems can occur.

To be able to visualize in rich detail, to be able to hold the image so steady you can copy off it, to be able to instantly access large amounts of information, is a skill so significantly valuable for succeeding in school. The students who do it have an easier time and do far better in school then the students who don't.

The shame is that it is a learnable skill and that it can make learning easier and more challenging. The additional benefit lies in the fact that the student KNOWS HOW to study <u>and</u> knows how to check if he knows something or not. Back in the old days (before television), kids listened to stories told by their elders or on radio and they made up the pictures because they had to in order to really enjoy the story (sound effects also helped). Now with TV, the pictures are ready made. I have had many students who do well in the classroom when the teacher visually presents the material and do poorly when the teacher does not. They simply did not know they were supposed to make up their own pictures and we (the teachers) did not know we were supposed to teach them to do it.

One last reason for teaching a visual learning strategy. Imagine having an audio tape of a class you were taking. You can remember the teacher talking about a particular topic, parts of which you could remember including the terms he used. If you wanted to access that information from the audio tape, you would have to do it <u>in a linear fashion</u>. That means you would have to play the tape from the first and listen to every word until you got to the terms you were listening for. Isn't that time consuming? Now imagine that you have the lecture stored as a detailed photograph or picture. As soon as you say the word or term to yourself and picture what it would be like, you would have instant access to the part of the lecture you were looking for. That is what a visual learning strategy offers. The old cliché that a "picture is worth a thousand words" is only a part of the power of the visual learning strategy. The fact that you have instant access to **any** part of the picture is what is really helpful to you as the student.

All of the above facts; that it makes learning easier, that it makes learning faster, that it makes learning more challenging, and that it is a missing skill for a significant number of students makes a compelling case for a massive drive to overcome this deficiency and to help these students develop this visual learning strategy.

ACADEMIC SKILLS FOR STUDENTS

Learning Spelling Words

Students are constantly asked to learn new spelling words and yet many are not taught a good strategy to do it. Many students are told to write the words five to ten times or to sound the words out phonetically. Sometimes this works but many times it does not. This section covers how to teach your child or student an extremely effective strategy for learning spelling words in an easy and fun way.

All excellent spellers have one trait in common. They spell a word off of a very clear internal picture of the word. So the question is "How do we teach other students to do that?" In order to help a student learn to spell using this new spelling strategy, it is important you lead him through these steps for each new spelling word:

1. Have the student write the word divided into syllables (e.g., <u>al</u> <u>bu</u> <u>quer</u> <u>que</u>). Then have him look at the new spelling word and REMEMBER WHAT IT LOOKS LIKE. If the word is long, make a picture of each syllable and then put all the pictures together.

2. Now from his internal image, have him spell the word **BACKWARDS** (from right to left) out loud to you. You check to make sure he spells it correctly. Have him do it several times.

3. Once he can spell it backwards (and only then), have him sound the word out **WHILE** looking at the internal image of the word. This "hooks" the sound of the word to the internal image of the word.

...have him sound the word out **WHILE** looking at the internal image of the word. This "hooks" the sound of the word to the internal image of the word.

4. Then have him spell it from left to right off of the internal image.

5. Praise him for his success and new skill. Go to the next spelling word and repeat steps 1 — 5.

After the above strategy has been completed on each of the spelling words (and after a period of time has passed), practice by picking random words off the spelling list and have the student spell them. After practicing a word six to eight times, the student should be able to just say the word, see the internal image and spell it correctly without having to spell it backwards. Practicing the spelling words over time (like a few days) will drop the correct spelling into long term memory.

Some additional tips and/or variations on using the spelling strategy are:

1. Get students into a visualizing mode by having them imagine something very familiar such as a friend, grandparent, pet, or movie star.

2. Before you launch into this spelling strategy with new and difficult words, teach them the strategy by spending one to two sessions having them learn to spell small and familiar words backwards. Gradually increase the size of the words until they are the same size and complexity as the words on their spelling list. Let them give you words to spell backwards so you can make it a game.

3. Some variations on step 1 of the spelling strategy are:
   a. Have the students look at the spelling word and write it down before they make an internal image.
   b. Have the students write the word in the air with their fingers on an

imaginary chalkboard.

c. While you slowly spell the word out loud, have the students "print it" in their minds' eye. You may have to repeat it several times.

d. When the words start to get longer, have them break the words down into syllables or miniwords (e.g., have them see the word *student* as <u>stu</u> <u>dent</u>).

Remember, the reason you have the students spell the word backwards is to assure yourself and the students that they have a clear internal image of that word. They cannot smoothly spell the word backwards unless they can see it clearly. Being able to see the word clearly in their minds' eye is the common trait of all excellent spellers. Also, as a student develops his ability to visualize the words, he can drop the process of spelling it backwards because he will learn to know when he has a good picture.

> ...the reason you have the students spell the word backwards is to assure yourself and the students that they have a clear internal image of that word.

Learning Vocabulary Words

Previously, I talked about the importance of students learning visually. In particular, I talked about students who sounded out words while reading and had very little comprehension when they got through reading because the sound of the word did not elicit an internal experience. When I teach a student to read, I want the sound of the word to elicit visual internal experiences. This is because visualizing enhances interest and comprehension.

In order for this to happen, a student must build a "visual vocabulary." This section is about how to do that. It is a different way to learn those definitions or vocabulary words that schools assign to the students to learn. Learning vocabulary words requires logical connections among the sight of the word, the sound of the word, and the meaning of the word. The meaning of the word needs to be represented primarily visually.

Learning vocabulary words requires logical connections among the sight of the word, the sound of the word, and the meaning of the word. The meaning of the word needs to be represented primarily visually.

The way to do this is as follows:

1. Read the definition of the word and form a visual representation of the **meaning** of the word. The picture can be realistic, symbolic or metaphoric; it can be very complex, a collage, or even a moving picture. It is important that every little nuance of the meaning be represented in the visual representation and that the picture accurately portrays all the subtle meanings of the word.

2. Somewhere in the visual representation, imbed the sight of the word being represented. Make the word nice and big and easily read. You can even make it a special color. If you have trouble imaging the word, spell it backwards a few times.

3. While looking at the picture of the word with an image of the word imbedded in it, sound out the word. It is **EXTREMELY IMPORTANT** to be looking at the picture while you simultaneously say the word. This simultaneous representation is what logically connects the sound and picture together.

4. Now, **while looking at the picture** with the word in it, say the word and describe the picture. Repeat this several times. If the teacher will let you define the word in your own words — do so. If, however, the teacher wants the definition verbatim, recite the exact definition while looking at the picture of the meaning of the word.

5. Practice step four, 6 - 8 times to drop it into long term memory.

The reason we go through all these steps is that we want the sound of the word and the sight of the word to "hook" the picture of the <u>meaning</u> of the word. This way when a student reads by subvocalizing or by sighting the words, a visual internal experience will be generated. Once a sufficient visual vocabulary has been built up, a student should find it easier and easier to read visually.

As I am teaching this process to a student, I use various examples of words of different kinds of meanings to illustrate the teaching point. The first example I use has become famous with my students because of my lousy artistic ability. However, they never forget the definition of the word. I promised all my students that this would be in my book so here goes!

One of the definitions of a horse given by the dictionary is "A horse is a large four-legged animal with hooves which we use to ride and pull wagons." I then point out to them to make sure to place certain items in the picture (like hooves, rider, and wagon) to remind them of certain words or phrases when they are having to recite the definition back to the teacher.

In my opinion, developing a visual vocabulary is one of the most important strategies to be learned. The lack of a good strategy is one of the biggest stumbling blocks to learning to read with comprehension and to success in school.

Most students attempt to learn vocabulary words by first reading the word then reading the definition. They repeat this process over and over. It is, by far, the most common method that students of ALL ages utilize when attempting to learn vocabulary words. It is ineffective, inefficient, boring, and tiresome, AND, it does not take the meaning of the words and overlap it into another sense. The meaning remains just a blob of words so that later, when the student is reading and runs across the word, the only experience his brain has of the word is a blob of MORE words.

Since most students naturally learn visually, their attempt at reading, therefore, leaves many HOLES in their internal images. They realize they don't know what they are reading and they get bored and give up.

Learning to Visually Read

In this section, we will cover how to visually read. That is, how to form pictures of the meaning of the words you are reading.

Practically everybody has had the experience of reading for a while then pausing and realizing they have no idea what they just read. The words just didn't register any place in the brain.

One reason this occurs is that many people read by sounding out the words (either out loud or inside their head) and the sound of the words do not "hook" an experience. Another reason this occurs is that the reader does not know what the reading material is about before he starts to read. This is similar to attempting to put a jigsaw puzzle together "face down" without benefit of the picture on the box. Each piece is there but there is nothing to guide you in how to put the pieces together. It would be, therefore, a boring and tedious task. What is needed is for the sounded out words to overlap into pictures in the brain. Then comprehension and interest can occur.

Visually reading is like putting together a jigsaw puzzle the correct way. Each word is a part of the picture and adjusts the picture according to its own meaning.

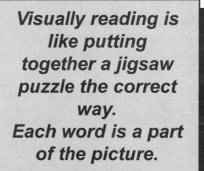

Visually reading is like putting together a jigsaw puzzle the correct way. Each word is a part of the picture.

To give my students a sense of what I am talking about, I give them the following experience: "Visually reading is like visually listening. In both instances, you hear words and overlap the meaning of the words into pictures. As more and more words come in, your mind adjusts the picture accordingly. To give you an example of this, I'm going to tell you a short story. I want you to make pictures of the story. This is a story about horses. so I want you to get a picture of six or seven horses in your mind. You don't know how to picture what they are doing yet because I haven't told you. Now, notice how your pictures change as I give you some more of the story.

This picture, like the jigsaw puzzle picture on the box, gives your brain guidance in how to piece together or form pictures of the meaning of the words. This is called "setting up" the reading in your brain.

The horses are running...So, you adjust the picture to make them run."

The horses are running very fast...So, if your horses were just trotting, you get them to gallop."

The horses are running very fast around the track...So, if you had them running in an open field you have to adjust the picture by putting a track into it."

The horses are running very fast around the track at Remington Park in Oklahoma City. Notice, if you have been to Remington Park, how much more realistic your picture is than when you had to make it up. If you haven't been there, you will have to store the name at some place in the picture."

It is opening day at Remington Park on September 1, 1989. Sometimes in school, you have to remember events and dates. So, how are you going to store and remember that it was opening day and the date. Many students will picture a banner with "OPENING DAY" and the date printed on it."

The first race is nearing an end and the crowd is on its feet cheering wildly. It is a bright and sunny day, the sky is blue and there are no clouds. The crowd is in summer clothes and is in a festive mood. The winner of the first race is a horse by the name of "Beetlebum." Now, where will you put the name of the horse in your story? On the side of the horse, on the race results board?"

The jockey's name is Sam Jones." Where are you going to put his name?"

After the race, the owners, Mr. and Mrs. Dale Wood of Colorado led the horse and jockey into the Winners Circle to receive a trophy from Gov. Bellmon." Think about where you are going to put all those names."

To help you remember this story, you immediately review the story in your head by going back and telling yourself everything you put in the picture — the banner with the opening day on it and the date, the name of the race track, the horse's name, jockey's name, owner's name, and the Governor's name. You tell yourself these names WHILE you are looking at the internal pictures. In fact, it even helps if you have a partial picture ahead of time of what the story or reading is "about." In the story, I told you it was about horses and to make a picture of six or seven horses. This picture, like the jigsaw puzzle picture on the box, gives your brain guidance in how to piece together or form pictures of the meaning of the words. This is called "setting up" the reading in your brain.

You "set up" the reading by getting an answer to the question "what is this reading material about?" You want the answer to be a sense and a partial picture — not a well formulated conclusion. You do this prior to reading the material by quickly scanning the material with the question in your mind. In fact, a better question which will also engage interest is, "What is this about <u>and</u> how is it important to me or how will I use it?" You can get an answer to this

...a better question which will also engage interest is, "What is this about <u>and</u> how is it important to me or how will I use it?

question by looking at pictures and illustrations, by scanning captions and headings, and/or by reading topical sentences of leading paragraphs. Setting up a reading should only take a few seconds. If you don't set it up in your mind before you start reading, it will feel like putting a jigsaw puzzle together FACE DOWN and without the picture to guide you.

Once you have a sense of what the material is about, you want to know how the author organizes the material. You can find this out if the author broke it down into major chapters or sections. After you have determined this, it will be important for your own comprehension and recall ability to image the reading material organized in your mind. In other words, image how the chapter is broken down into sections, then how each section is broken down. Image what each breakdown is about and then start reading about each smaller section. After a section is read, connect those pictures to the other imaged sections.

Steps of the Reading Strategy
1. Set it up in your mind by getting an answer to the question "What is this about?"
2. Find out how the author breaks the content down.
3. Visually read it.
4. Review with words the internal images you made WHILE looking at the pictures.
5. Practice the review of step 4 over time to drop it into long term memory.

Once you have a sense of what the reading is about in the form of a collection of pictures, you proceed to visually read by filling in the details of the pictures or by adjusting the pictures according to the words you read. When you run across data you need to remember such as names, dates or places, simply insert the data in the picture in a logical spot. By the time you get through reading you may have multiple pictures in a sequence or collage.

You can also turn it into a movie. It seems to help the memory if you will periodically stop and review the internal images and tell yourself what is in the pictures including all data. Do this in the form of a narrative or story if at all possible. If any part of the picture or any of the data is unclear, go back and clear up the picture even if it means spelling it backwards. Be sure you do this WHILE looking at the pictures.

For the knowledge to become a part of long term memory, the review may need to occur 6 - 8 times over a period of time. The longer the period of time you review it, the more long term the memory.

To tie the visual reading strategy to the importance of the visual vocabulary, I tell my students the "Zit Story". I give them a easy set of instructions and tell them to visualize doing them. The instructions may be, "Stand up and go over to the door, with your left hand open the door and step out into the hallway, see who is there, step back into the office and with your right hand close the door, then come over to me and report what you saw in the hallway." They usually do this quite easily.

I then say to them, "I want you to have an experience of what it is like to not be able to visualize words. So, I'm going to give you another set of instructions but this time I'm going to say the word "zit" when I want you to not be able to visualize the meaning of the word. Notice what happens to your pictures." I then give them a set of instructions such as, "Go over to the zit zit and zit a zit. Reach in and pull out the zit zit. With the zit in your zit hand, zit over to the zit and zit zit."

They usually look at me with a blank look on the face. I also remind them that is how they looked when they didn't know what they had read. This is what the instructions would have been like if I had not put zits in. "Go over to the file cabinet and open a drawer. Reach in and pull out the student file. With the file in your left hand, come over to the chair and sit down." They obviously visualize it very easily this time.

Then I say, "What this means is, if you don't use my strategy in learning your vocabulary words, you are going to get zits when you read!" Teenagers get the point.

Learning Math Facts

Memorizing math facts, (particularly multiplication and short division) is one task that many elementary students find very boring and tiresome. One of the reasons for this is that many students attempt to memorize the tables by repeating them over and over to themselves or out loud. This repetitive behavior is, by it's very nature, boring and tiresome. Many students quit trying and never learn their math facts which hampers them in future math courses — even into college.

The following is a way to learn math facts which is different and more appealing to students — primarily because it is visual and can be made into a game. The process can be taught to a large group, small groups, or one-on-one. However, since participation by each student is crucial to that child's learning the math facts, small groups or one-on-one is recommended.

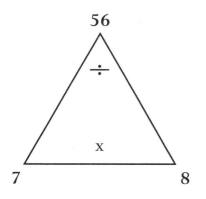

Have the student fill in a triangle, like the one on the left, with each math fact they are supposed to learn. You or another student teach the math fact to the student in the following manner:

1. Hold the triangle in front of the student so she has a good image of the triangle. Be sure to note which corner has which number in it. Have her trace the triangle with her eyes noting the position of each element (including the multiplication and division signs).

2. Now lay the triangle down and trace the image of the triangle in the air and point to each of the five elements until the student can call out the position of each of the elements of the triangle from her memory of the image.

3. Using your finger as a pointer, visually sequence the math facts (both multiplication and short division) while she calls out the facts. For example:

> 7 times 8 = 56,
> 56 divided by 7 = 8,
> 8 times 7 = 56,
> 7 divided into 56 = 8,
> 56 divided by 8 = 7,
> 8 divided into 56 = 7.

Have the student continue until she can respond without any hesitation. It'sextremely important that the child call out the answer even if she has to do it slowly. You should trace the sequence slowly at first and then gradually speed up.

4. Change to another math fact and repeat the process.

If the student has to learn all the multiplication/short division facts, I have her systematically work through them in the following fashion:

Start with a 9 in the lower right hand of the triangle and a 9 in the lower left hand. Of course the top is 81. Do the process in step 3. Then change the 9 in the left hand corner of the triangle to an 8 — the top is now 72. The lower right remains a 9. Do the process in step 3. After about 5 new math facts are learned in this manner, go over and over the facts to help make the answer automatic. You may also use flash cards with the new math facts for a few minutes.

Systematically change the lower left hand until you get to the zero so that you will have covered all multiplication and short division facts involving the number 9. After adding the second five facts, practice all math facts from previous lessons. This review and practice over time will habituate the math facts and allow them to drop into long term memory.

Then change the 9 in the lower right hand corner to an 8 and systematically work through all the numbers in the lower left hand corner until you have finished the eights. Continuing changing the lower right hand corner until you have covered all the multiplication and short division facts.

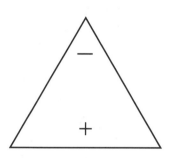

It is also easy to learn the additions and subtraction facts using the triangle concept. You adjust the triangle to look like the one to the left and systematically work through the desired math facts in the same manner as the multiplication and division facts. DO NOT attempt to learn multiplication/division and addition/subtraction at the same time.

With either multiplication/division or addition/subtraction facts, it is very important to use flash cards or to have speed contests over time so the math facts will become automatic and drop into long term memory. The longer the period of time they are practiced, the longer term their memory will be.

Another suggestion, particularly for the additions and subtractions, is to start with the larger numbers and work down. For one thing, this impresses them, but more importantly, it keeps them from using their fingers and counting or otherwise trying some of their old systems.

Making ANY Subject Interesting

Many students complain that certain subjects are not interesting and even boring. Making any subject or lesson interesting is a necessary skill for successful students. If you can't do this as a student, you are dependent on those instances when a teacher makes the "right" statement that "turns you on" to something. This places too much responsibility on the teacher and leaves too much to chance.

Three basic elements make a lesson interesting. First, it has to relate to "something" in a way that makes sense. Second, that "something" has to be important to the student. Third, the lesson to be learned needs to be stored in the brain in a way the student finds interesting (e.g., to be displayed visually). For most students, the third element will be taken care of when they learn to visualize their lessons. The first element is taken care of when they "set up" their lesson by getting an answer to the question "What is this about?" (this was covered under Visual Reading). This section is about how we find out what is important to the student and how to relate the different lessons to it.

> Three basic elements make a lesson interesting. First, it has to relate to "something" in a way that makes sense. Second, that "something" has to be important to the student. Third, the lesson to be learned needs to be stored in the brain in a way the student finds interesting

One way to find out what is important to the students is to do the following:
1. Survey their subjects in school, their activities in school and out of school (even hobbies and sports), and list the ones in which they are naturally interested.

2. Get an answer to one or more of the following questions about the interesting subjects or activities:
   ♦ "What is it about the activity that they find so important?"
   ♦ "What does the activity do for them?"
   ♦ "What do they like or find interesting about the activity?"

You can guess the answers or ask them directly. If you ask them directly, be genuinely interested, nonjudgmental, and very curious.

3. Listen for criteria or standards. Listen for "what is **REALLY** important to them about it." Be sure you listen with an open mind rather than impose your own criteria or standards on them or what you think the criteria should be.

> You can guess the answers or ask them directly. If you ask them directly, be genuinely interested, nonjudgmental, and very curious.

4. Once you have the answers (there may be more than one criterion that the activity satisfies), search for the way a particular lesson, school subject, homework, or school can satisfy the criteria and point out the connection to them. Do it in a curious, helpful, and interested manner and tone. Be sure and not get into an argument about whether or not the connection is right or wrong. If you do, it won't connect.

5. If you can't make the connection with the criterion you are using, "chunk up". Ask the questions in 2. above about the criterion you were just using. The answers will give you even higher valued criteria — which will have more importance for them. Now try 4. again with the new criterion. You can continue "chunking up" until you can make the connection.

Now when they are "setting up" a lesson in their mind in preparation to studying, expand the original question of "what is this about?' to any of the following:

♦ "What is this lesson about and how does it relate to what's important to me (my criteria)?"

♦ "What is this lesson about and where will I use it?"

♦ "What is this lesson about and what will learning this do for me?"

When they get a satisfactory answer, interest is activated. If they or you can't yet find an answer to any of the questions, they have a legitimate reason not to be interested.

Test and Performance Anxiety

Test or performance anxiety can range from a mild case of the butterflies, which quickly goes away once the test or performance has begun, to a raging phobia which completely blocks a successful test or performance. The following exercise will and can help most students, performers and/or athletes get relief from this phenomena.

I am going to write these instructions as though you, the reader, were here in front of me in my office. This way, if you are leading someone else through this exercise, you can simply read the instructions to him or her.

1. Think of a couple of recent times you have had test or performance anxiety. Allow yourself to get back into the anxiety. Not too much — just enough so that you remember and know what it feels like.

2. Now allow your mind to drift back in time and see if you can remember the first time you encountered this test or performance anxiety. If you can't tell for sure if it was the first time, find the time you had the most anxiety. When you have found the memory, put that memory aside for a moment and get up and walk around to allow your body and mind to calm down.

3. Now imagine yourself sitting in a movie theater with a large screen in front of you. In a moment, you are going to play a movie of the anxiety memory in step 2. For now put a scene prior to the memory on the screen and **freeze it** (for example, it may be of you walking into the classroom). Do not play the movie until we are through setting up the exercise.

4.   Now imagine yourself up in the projection booth of the movie theater watching yourself sitting in the theater while at the same time watching yourself on the movie screen. When you can do this, allow the movie of the

anxiety memory play on the screen. Be sure you maintain the double image of you seeing yourself watching yourself on the screen. Play the movie to the end of the anxiety memory and past it to where you are feeling better and then freeze the last frame of the movie.

5. Change the quality of the movie to that of an old movie you might see on TV — black and white with streaks of light flitting through it. Start circus music playing on the sound track of the movie and replay the movie backwards while you are associated back into your body. In other words, imagine you are in the last frame of the anxiety memory, and you start replaying the anxiety memory **BACKWARDS** as black and white with flicks of light and with circus music playing in the background. You and other people will walk backwards, etc.

6. When you have completed the task, get up and walk around for a moment to let your mind and body settle back to normal.

7. Now test yourself by allowing yourself to go back to that anxiety memory you chose in step 2 and relive it in your mind. Notice any changes you have in the anxiety level. Also notice the curiously detached feeling you have about the incident.

8. What feelings do you want to have when you are about to perform or be tested? Choose several that are the most useful to you and allow yourself to re-experience them. Most people choose confidence, competence, calmness, relaxed, etc.

9. Now replay the anxiety memory with the new feelings which you want to have on tests or performances. Is that how you want to feel?

10. If so, think of the next few times you are going to have a test or performance and vividly imagine yourself going through it with the feelings you chose in step 8.

11. If your anxiety is gone in step 10 and you can access the new feelings you chose — congratulations and go do well. If you have some anxiety left, sometimes it helps to repeat the process starting with step 3 or going back to step 1.

Remembering To Do Things

A common complaint I hear from parents is that their child forgets to bring books or homework home from school or to turn completed homework in to the teacher. How to remember to do things **WHEN** you want to do them is a useful skill to have — even for us older adults.

In general, remembering to do things when you want to do them involves two elements:

1. You need to have an internal experience of what you want to remember to do, and
2. You need to "hook" that internal experience to a **reliable** external cue that will let you know it is time to do it.

Internal experience means you have a combination of pictures, sounds, feelings, muscle sensations, smells or tastes of the thing to do.

So, for example, if you wanted to remember to bring home a book from school, you could make a picture of yourself picking up the book, tell yourself to get the book, and/or feel the muscle sensations of picking up the book. It works best if you will pick at least two of the senses. Suppose you picked telling yourself to "pick up the book" and feeling the "sensation of picking up the book". It is important to do them together or simultaneously since that is what connects them together in the brain. You now have an internal experience of picking up a book.

You now want it connected to a reliable external cue. The cue can be something you see, hear, feel, smell or taste. Since we used hearing and feeling for the internal experience, let's pick something visual for the external cue. It could be when you see the teacher dismissing the class — but you might forget by the time you get to your locker. So, let's pick walking up to the locker with the book in it because we know you are going to do that. So now, **SIMULTANEOUSLY** form an image of yourself walking up to the locker with the book in it, while telling yourself "pick up the book", while feeling the "sensation of picking up the book". In other words, do all three of them at the same time and practice the connection several times. You have now connected the internal experience to an external cue.

Recently, I was working with a young man who kept forgetting to bring his social studies book when he came to see me. According to his mother, it was a common occurrence to forget to bring books and homework home. So I decided to teach him this remembering strategy. I had him form a picture of himself reaching into his school locker and pulling out his book while **AT THE SAME TIME** he was imagining how the book would feel in his hand. Imagining the picture and muscle sensation simultaneously is critical because that is what hooks them together. He practiced this connection several times to strengthen it. At that point in time he had an internal experience of picking up his social studies book.

I then asked him for something unique that happened when he was coming to see me instead of going home. He indicated that his Dad picked him up and would come to him and say "time to go". Since we used visual and feeling for internal experience, we picked auditory for the external cue. So he **SIMULTANEOUSLY** saw himself picking up the book and felt the muscle sensation while hearing his Dad say "time to go". After practicing the connection a few times he was finished. When he walked into my office the next time, he proudly waved the book and said, "I remembered the book and I didn't even have to do

"I remembered the book and I didn't even have to do anything — it just popped into my mind."

anything — it just popped into my mind."

This remembering strategy works very well with about anything. The critical points are:

1. To create the thing to be remembered in internal experiences in two of the senses.

2. To select an external cue in another sense which is reliable.

3. To connect them all together by simultaneously representing them.

4. Practice the connections a few times.

Memorizing Facts and Data

One of the most common academic skills students need to survive school is the ability to store and retrieve information and data in a way so they can score well on tests. Common pieces of information that students are required to remember AT LEAST until test time include dates of various events such as when Columbus discovered America or the date of the signing of the Constitution, etc. Many students have no way of knowing for sure that they know the information or they have VERY inadequate ways of storing and retrieving the information.

In order to remember something, you must know:

1. Where you are going to put the information, and
2. How to retrieve it **WHEN** you want to retrieve it.

Where you are going to put the information can be limited to five choices — your five senses; visual, auditory, kinesthetic (muscle memory or emotion), smell or taste. Smell and taste are not very useful in the classroom, so let's concentrate on visual, auditory, and kinesthetic.

Kinesthetic is useful for typing, sports, auto mechanics, etc. but not too useful in the classroom because it is too slow. Auditory is useful for drama, speech making, singing, etc. Many students try to learn auditorially by repeating information over and over. The disadvantage of this is twofold. It is boring and slow. Visual is the best place to store information from the classroom or a book. It is fast and interesting to the students of today who were brought up on TV and movies.

So, let's practice on the story about Columbus discovering America. Picture in your mind's eye an ocean and a sandy beach. You can embellish the picture with animals, trees, sea gulls, clouds, color, motion, wind, etc. — anything to make it interesting. Now imagine a group of men standing on the beach, in funny dress, planting a flag in the sand. Also, picture three sailing ships anchored off the shore in the ocean. Now, zoom into the picture in your mind close to the leader of the men who has the flag and picture his name printed across his chest -- Columbus. Picture it vividly — spell it backwards if you need to. Now look at the flag and notice that it has a date and a country name on it — Spain, 1492. This is the country from which Columbus sailed and the year he sailed. Now look out in the harbor and zoom in next to one of the three ships where the name of the ship would be and notice that the ship's name is Pinta. Do the same for the next ship — Nina. The third ship's name is Santa Maria. Picture each of them vividly.

Now, for the retrieval system. Since so many of our classrooms and tests are auditory. I want you to attach the sound of each of the names to its corresponding part in the picture. You do this by saying the word or date **WHILE** looking at the word or date. This logically connects the sound to the picture. This way when the test question or teacher says the word "Columbus", for example, the picture with all the answers in it will pop up in your mind. Practice pulling up the picture and describing it several times and it will drop into long term memory.

In every situation in which you are memorizing data, visualize the contextual setting and embed the facts and data in the picture in logical places. By telling yourself what is in the picture, you will automatically retrieve the pictures when you read the test question.

Test Taking

Many students study hard for a test and think they know the material. When they go in to take the test, however, they "blank out" and can't seem to remember the answers. There are many possible reasons for this.

Many students study hard for a test and think they know the material. When they go in to take the test, however, **they "blank out" and can't seem to remember the answers.**

One, is that when they studied the students had not stored the data and information in the visual field and when they tried to answer the question they accessed the visual field and it wasn't there. The phrase "blank out" indicates that. Most often, in this kind of situation, the students have auditorially studied. That means they repeated the material over and over in an attempt to learn it. Another way to auditorially learn is by discussing it with another person or by having another person grill you on it by asking you questions — over and over.

Another reason some students think they study hard for a test and then don't do well is the way they review. They go over and over their notes and/or textbook laboriously by reading and re-reading the material. Many times they are just saying the words to themselves and the words are not going into their mind and creating an experience. Therefore, they feel that they studied hard but in fact it was a very ineffective strategy — it did not contribute to their knowledge or their confidence.

Therefore, they feel that they studied hard but in fact it was a very ineffective strategy — it did not contribute to their knowledge or their confidence.

Another possible reason is the structure and nature of the questions. Multiple choice tests many times force students into an auditory mode for answering the questions when, in fact, the answers are visually learned. An example of this is when students read all the choices for answers and select the one which "sounds the best." Even study guides for taking multiple choice tests suggest that you read all the answers, then eliminate the two most obvious answers, then choose the answer from the remaining choices. This is a lot of reading of material that is irrelevant. Later on, I will share a strategy for taking multiple choice tests.

> Multiple choice tests many times force students into an auditory mode for answering the questions when, in fact, the answers are visually learned.

A final reason is that the student has a test phobia or at least a high level of test anxiety. If he hasn't studied enough and/or effectively, the anxiety may be justified. Some students, however, have developed test anxieties that won't go away no matter how well they have studied. These anxieties paralyze their minds and they cannot take the test to the best of their ability. They sometimes panic and can even make themselves physically sick. How to deal with test anxieties and phobias is dealt with in another section of this book.

When I coach students on preparing for tests, the first thing I want to make sure of is that they have an effective learning strategy. I want to know that the information and understanding is in their mind. Since, I obviously believe in visual learning, I want to make sure they learn the material visually. The second thing I check on is how they review for tests. Many students review their notes and book auditorially as previously noted. I coach the student to review the pictures they have made in their mind while they were studying. If they can ask the question "What was this about?", get their mind into the subject matter, and pull up all the pictures with the embedded names, facts, etc, they can relax because they already know the material. This is a way to "KNOW WHEN YOU KNOW IT." If they find holes in their pictures or if they are unclear, then they need to go back and review their notes and/or textbook and make new pictures.

If they can ask the question "What was this about?", get their mind into the subject matter, and pull up all the pictures with the embedded names, facts, etc, they can relax because they already know the material. This is a way to "KNOW WHEN YOU KNOW IT."

The strategy I teach my students for taking a **multiple choice test** is as follows:

1) Read the test question,
2) Ask yourself "What is the question about?" and get an internal image of the material,
3) Find the answer to the question in the internal image, and
4) Determine which of the multiple choice answers best matches your conclusion.

This strategy keeps you in the visual field where you stored the information when you studied. You are saving time because it keeps you from having to read irrelevant material. It also rescues you from the old auditory reading pattern where you just sound out the words and try to force understanding.

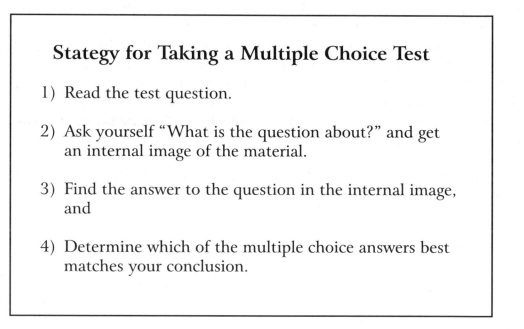

Stategy for Taking a Multiple Choice Test

1) Read the test question.

2) Ask yourself "What is the question about?" and get an internal image of the material.

3) Find the answer to the question in the internal image, and

4) Determine which of the multiple choice answers best matches your conclusion.

How to Take Notes

Often I find that the way students attempt to take notes during class interferes with their learning experience. When a student is listening in class, I want him to build an internal visual experience of what the teacher is saying. I want him to build vivid pictures of the **meaning** of the words the teacher is using. If the student can kinesthetically associate into the pictures, then it is even better. Kinesthetically associating means the student sees himself active in the picture and feels the muscle and/or emotional sensations of the activity. To do this, he needs to overlap the words into action pictures and focus on the pictures and kinesthetics instead of the words.

Many students, however, spend most of their time in class taking copious notes. Some try to write down practically everything the teacher is saying or at least everything the teacher writes on the board. This forces their minds to focus on the words the teacher is saying and, if they are not careful, interferes with the overlapping into pictures and kinesthetics. It also "plugs up" some of the information the teacher is continuing to put out. This is because most people, when writing down a sentence, will internally repeat the sentence in either the teacher's voice or their own voice. The effect of this is that they can't hear what the teacher is saying while they are in internal dialogue with themselves. This is because they can't consciously hear two or more things at the same time. They, therefore, have missing information.

> This is because most people, when writing down a sentence, will internally repeat the sentence in either the teacher's voice or their own voice. The effect of this is that they can't hear what the teacher is saying while they are in internal dialogue with themselves.

The **note taking strategy** I teach my students is as follows:

1) Set the lecture up in your mind ahead of time and get a beginning picture of "what the lecture is about".

2) Listen to the teacher's words and overlap them into pictures of what they mean.

3) If the teacher says something profound that needs to be memorized or reviewed, summarize the idea with a code word or two and insert it in your internal picture. When you can, such as when the teacher pauses, write the code word down while you are continuing to visualize the material.

4) After the lecture is over, go back and look at the code word and recall the pictures and review or memorize the material. If a "hard copy" of the material is needed or wanted, write the description of the pictures down as you review the lecture. This will give you the notes to study later, and strengthen your memory.

Developing a Positive Attitude About School and Learning

Many students do not have a proper attitude toward school and learning and it gets in the way of enjoying school. If your mind does not know how to think positively **about** whatever it is you are engaged in, then you tend to be disinterested and easily distracted. It's kind of like having the picture on the box of a jigsaw puzzle to guide you in the selection of the pieces. The picture makes the game more interesting and easier to do.

If the way you think about something is positive, your interest tends to become engaged. If you

> If your mind does not know how to think positively **about** whatever it is you are engaged in, then you tend to be disinterested and easily distracted.

think about it in a negative way, you are turned off or disinterested. The way to elicit the attitude of a student toward school is to ask them "What is the purpose of school to you?" or "Why do you go to school?" Many students will answer "I don't know!" or "Because my parents make me!" or "Because the law makes me!" or many will just shrug their shoulders and say "I don't know." The students who answer this way will typically be bored, turned off of school or even rebellious. Even students who give a more logical answer are not necessarily turned on to school because of their answer. For example, "I go to school so I can get a good job." or "I go to school so I will be a good citizen." Even the answer "I go to school so I can be with my friends." doesn't help motivate the student with doing their school work.

Over the years, I have developed the following story to tell to my students. The story gives them a way to think about learning and school that is tied to their identity at a deep level. It is tied to their identity in a natural way — their reason for being here and alive on this planet Earth. I then proceed to describe a way to think about each of their courses they are currently taking. The effect of this is that it ties who they are as a person to who they are as a lifelong learner, to how to think about school, to how to think about each of their subjects, to how to learn each subject. The story, as though told to a student, goes like this:

The Story

Have you ever thought about the fact that when you were first born that you couldn't do anything for yourself? Oh, you could breathe, you could suck and swallow, you could make some unintelligible sounds, and you could dirty your diapers, but that's about all. Your mother and father had to do most things for you. Then as you gained strength and observed things around you, you started doing some things for yourself.

You got to where you could lift your head and look around. Then you got to where you could get your elbows under you so you could lift your head higher. Then you started rolling over and edging forward — the beginning of movement. After a while, you had to be carefully watched because you were becoming mobile. Then you started crawling. Then you started pulling yourself up and attempting to stand. Of course, your parents were very encouraging and kept helping you practice these new skills. One day, you took your first step — then several steps — then very rapidly you were toddling — then walking — then running. Now you can run and throw or catch a ball at the same time. Pretty amazing development for such a little person.

Now the reason you were learning all of these things were so **you could learn to get along in the world**. So, you could physically move from one place to another. Now, originally your world was very small, but it was and is still rapidly expanding — as it should.

Another way **you learned to get along in the world**, was by learning to talk. At first, your cries sounded the same. Then you started having different cries or sounds for when you were hungry to when you needed your diaper changed to when you were uncomfortable. After a while you could babble. Then you started making noises that sounded like words. As you practiced these sounds, you became more and more intelligible and you started speaking in simple sentences. With these communication skills you could now **get along in the world** even better by interacting with others.

You were a fantastic learning organism. Everything that went on around you was soaked up and learned. You were designed by God **to learn how to get along in this world**. And, you do it very well. And, as you look back on that experience, aren't you glad that that little toddler didn't quit when she fell down a few times. Aren't you proud of the fact that she persevered and kept practicing, confident that she would learn it sooner or later. What would your life be like now if that little baby had given up when things got tough? That baby knew a lot about what it took **to learn to get along in the world**.

> You were designed by God **to learn how to get along in this world**. And, you do it very well.

We can probably still learn from that early experience. Because **you are still learning to get along in the world**. You are just learning at a different level — on a more complicated level — which is as it should be. And, you are still defining for yourself what getting along in the world means to you. It may mean that you want to be successful — as a professional or a person. It may mean that you want to have a lot of friends or to have a loving family or to have lots of money. But in order for you to accomplish that goal, whatever you choose for it to be, you have to do the same thing that little toddler did — **YOU HAVE TO LEARN HOW TO GET ALONG IN THE WORLD.**

Now, many years ago, somebody decided that they didn't want the upcoming young people to have to rediscover the learnings that had taken place before their time. That would waste too much time. They wanted a way to speed up the process. So that you could, as quickly as possible, learn all the accumulated knowledge and then go on and live your life — to **get along in the world in whatever way you chose**. So they invented school. A major purpose for school is to provide a place and a way to dump the accumulated knowledge and wisdom of the world into your brain so you can go out and do your thing. So you wouldn't have to reinvent the wheel, so to speak. And to do it as rapidly as possible. Unfortunately, we don't have a Spock of Star Trek to do a "mind meld" on you. We sometimes wish we did.

> **A major purpose for school is to provide a place and a way to dump the accumulated knowledge and wisdom of the world into your brain so you can go out and do your thing.**

In lieu of that, we looked around and said "If we want them to be able to get along in the world, they need to know about the world! So, we will teach them the accumulated knowledge about the world in the form of subjects.

So, we look around the world and we notice the physical aspects of it. We notice the wind, the weather, the rocks, gravity, etc. and we decide we will have a course on the processes and rules and laws that govern the makeup of the physical world. We call this subject "Physical Science." And, since it is in the world, we need to learn it so we can use it **to learn how to get along in the world**.

Then, we notice that there are living things in the world. There are birds, animals, insects, fish, humans, and plants of all sorts. We notice that they are built differently and we wonder how they work and function. What are the processes that make them work? How do they function? We call this course "Live Science." And, since it is in the world, we need to learn it so we can use it **to learn how to get along in the world**.

We notice we have a history, a tradition, and we wonder how we got to where we are? What were the course of events which caused our civilization to evolve to the place where we are today? Can we learn anything from this history so that, perhaps, we might learn from any mistakes we may have made? We call this course of study "History". And, since it is in the world, we need to learn it so we can use it **to learn how to get along in the world**.

We notice there are other kinds of terrain and people. Different cultures in different countries do things differently. We wonder how they are different and how much like us are they and where are they located? We wonder how they survive and operate. What is their weather like? We call this course of study "Geography." And, since it is in the world, we need to learn it so we can use it **to learn how to get along in the world**.

Then we notice that people are trying to communicate with each other. They communicate with words by speaking or writing. They take in communication by listening or reading. In order for good and effective communication to take place certain rules have to be followed by both the giver of communication and the receiver. If they don't follow the same rules, it would be like a soccer and a baseball team trying to play each other on the same field at the same time — each using its own rules. The result would be total chaos.

The rules we learn in communication are the "rules of grammar." We also learn to speak and to write using these rules. We then learn to read by these rules when we learn to read Literature. We call this course of study "Language Arts" or "English."   And, since it is in the world, we need to learn it so we can use it **to learn how to get along in the world**.

We also learn that there are quantities in the world. How much you weigh or how tall you are or how much you make on your job or in your allowance or how fast something is going. Numbers are the measure of these quantities. And since we need to solve problems in the world involving these quantities, we need to know how to manipulate numbers. That is, we need to know how to count, add, subtract, multiply and divide these numbers so that we can solve problems in the world. We may want to compute the effect of a 15% raise, or we may want to take an inventory, or we may want to calculate the arrival time of a plane, or we may want to take a spaceship to Mars.

In all of these cases, we have to be able to manipulate numbers, or their representatives called letters, in order to solve these problems. We call this course of study "Mathematics." And, since quantities and numbers and problems represented by those quantities are in the world, we need to learn it so we can use it **to learn how to get along in the world**.

So, every time you take a new course in school, you ask yourself the question "What is this course the study of and is it in the world?" If the answer is YES, then you need to learn it so you can use it **to learn how to get along in the world**. This is a way to give meaning to every course you take.

"What is this course the study of and is it in the world?" If the answer is YES, then you need to learn it so you can use it **to learn how to get along in the world**. This is a way to give meaning to every course you take.

How To Learn Mathematics

There are several major stumbling blocks for many students attempting to learn math that rarely are dealt with or explained to the students. First, math not only requires the ability to conceptualize and understand, but it also requires the building of skills. In fact, math is much like learning a sport in that you start with very small skills like adding and subtracting numbers to more complicated skills like multiplying numbers before moving on to short and long division. Each additional skill requires the mastery of the preceding skill.

Much of the problems most students have in some math topics is not that they can't understand the concept but that they struggle so much with doing the basic skills they have not yet mastered. They don't have the time or energy to address the new concepts or more complicated skills because they have to stop and count on their fingers or work out a simple multiplication fact.

> **They will complain "I know how to do it, so why do I have to do 25 to 30 problems?"**

In fact, the major complaint which students have about studying math is that they have to do "all that homework!" They will complain, "I know how to do it, so why do I have to do 25 to 30 problems?" They deserve an answer. The reason is so they will develop that mastery of the underlying skill. You want that skill to become automatic. The first place this usually shows up is in the memorization of the math facts. You need to have instant recall of the math facts — in subtraction, addition, multiplication and short division.

One of the ways I get this across is by comparing it to some sport — hopefully a sport they play. I will ask them if they would be as good a baseball hitter, for example, if I just showed them how to bat and then let them take only a few swings or if I would let them take 25 swings in batting practice every day. Of course, they would be better with lots of practice because that makes the skill automatic. The same is true in learning the basic underlying math facts.

A second stumbling block is that most students don't know how to "think about" math in a way that makes it interesting and comprehensible. If you ask them why they study math, the answers range from "I don't know" to "I can use it to make change or balance my checkbook" to "It's required." It is my experience that knowing how to think about a subject sets up the mind to be able to comprehend the subject and can make the subject more interesting. Not having a subject set up in his or her mind is akin to putting together a jigsaw puzzle **FACE DOWN** and without the picture to guide you — boring, time consuming, and tedious! And, isn't that the way many students feel about math?

A third major stumbling block is related to the details that have to go into solving a math problem. This necessary requirement is distasteful to many students because they do it so slowly. They do it slowly partially because they haven't mastered the previous skills.

So, let us discuss how to think about Mathematics. In the previous section on "Making School Interesting", we discussed the notion that we go to school to learn how to get along in the world and that if a phenomena was in the world, then we need to learn about it.

So, there is a quantified part of our world, is there not? And, those quantities are measured by numbers. Your weight is measured by a number. You are a specific age measured by a number. You buy things with money measured by a number. Mathematics is the study of how to manipulate those numbers in order to solve quantitative problems which exist in the world.

First we learn how to manipulate numbers by learning how to count them. Then we learn how to add, subtract, multiply, and divide those numbers. Then we move on to more sophisticated and complicated processes. We then move on to using those processes to solve problems in the world that involve quantities.

So in the final analysis, **Mathematics is the study of the manipulation of numbers in order to solve quantitative problems in the world**. Of course, in higher mathematics the numbers are represented by letters and the problems are more abstract and complex.

You learn to count and add so you can learn how many apples you have just bought. You learn to multiply so you can compute how much they cost. You learn Calculus so you can compute the volume of the apple. It goes on and on.

If you will examine a math book, you will notice a pattern which will give you a clue as to how to study math. The authors will start off every chapter or new section with terminology or definitions and introduce the new math concept. They may introduce what a fraction is, or a decimal, or a complex number, or a algebraic expression. Learn this terminology or these definitions visually using the Vocabulary Strategy.

Next, they will teach you how to manipulate those concepts. They will cover how to add, subtract, multiply, and divide them. Then they introduce the idea of where they are useful in the world to solve problems and cover how to solve those problems. Then they give you the problems in the real world to practice on — called word problems. Then the next chapter or section repeats the whole process.

Since Math is the study of how to solve quantitative problems, one of the ways to organize it in your mind is in a series of internal pictures. The picture would represent the various kinds of quantitative problems which exist in the world. Within each picture you would also have the way to solve the problem. The form of the picture would look like the illustration on the right.

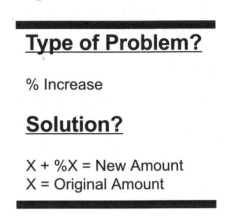

Type of Problem?

% Increase

Solution?

X + %X = New Amount
X = Original Amount

So, for example, if you were studying percentage increase problems, you would answer the first question with: "Percentage Increase Problems." Under the second question, you could enter a formula, or examples of how to solve the problems — or both. The formula for a percentage increase problem might look like: **X + %X = New amount (where X represents the original amount).** So the completed picture in your head would look like the second figure. Other ways to represent the kind of problem would be to have real life scenes superimposed in the picture. Examples for a percentage increase problem could be having to compute a pay raise, having to compute the mark-up to arrive at a retail price for a shirt in a clothing store.

After you have completed the internal picture it is important to tell yourself what is in the picture **WHILE LOOKING AT THE PICTURE**. This connects the auditory to the picture. Then when you are taking an exam, if after reading the test question you will ask yourself "What kind of problem is this?", the picture will pop up in your mind as soon as you answer it — complete with the method of solving it.

This is useful in solving word problems. In Algebra, when you are learning to solve mixture problems, for example, take the definition of a mixture problem and form a mental image symbolic of it. Since the definition is **"Any problem where two or more quantities are combined to produce a different quantity, or where a single quantity is separated into two or more different quantities,"** a mental image might be of two different pictures. One is where you are mixing liquids from two different beakers. The other is an image of you pouring liquid from a larger beaker into two smaller beakers. Somewhere in the image put the words "mixture problems."

Type of Problem?

Mixture Problem

Solution?

(%) Quantity$_1$ + (%) Quantity$_2$ = (%)Total.

Now somewhere in the image, place the form of the normal equation used to solve mixture problems: **(%) Quantity$_1$ + (%) Quantity$_2$ = (%)Total**. Now insert in your image several examples of different applications.

When you are trying to figure out how to solve a problem, look for common patterns in the solutions. They may be patterns in the typical way to set up the equation, or in setting up the variables. There will always be these patterns that make learning how to solve the kind of problem easier. If there are formulas or diagrams store those in the image also.

Once you have the common patterns stored in the image, look for exceptions or variations in the solutions. Store those in the image in a like type manner. Now that all this information has been stored in an image and the image has been encoded under a specific "Kind of Problem", review off of your internal image a auditory description of the image. Tell yourself the kind of problem, how to solve it, and any exceptions or variations to watch for. By auditorially reviewing it **while looking at the internal image**, you logically connect the internal image and auditory track. This gives you an auditory backup system to the image. It also gives you auditory access to the visual image. Which means, as stated earlier, that when taking a test, if you will ask yourself "What kind of problem is this?" after you have read the test question, the answer in the form of the image will pop up in your mind.

One of the better ways for the beginning student to learn to store information in their internal images is by learning to visualize the information in their mind and spelling or saying it BACKWARDS (from right to left). The purpose of doing this is to assure the student that he or she has a good image. You cannot smoothly spell or say something backwards in any way other than visually so it assures the student that the information is stored in the image. For example, the distance formula between two points P_1 and P_2 is given by: **d = the square root of ($(X_2 - X_1)^2 + (Y_2 - Y_1)^2$).** By visualizing and saying it backwards, you would recite: **Under the square root — squared-close parenthesis-sub1-Y-minus-sub2-Y-open parenthesis-plus-squared-close parenthesis-sub 1-X-minus-sub 2- X- open parenthesis-is equal to the distance between two points P_1 and P_2.**

One of the math courses that creates a great deal of agony for many students is **GEOMETRY**. It seems that many very bright math students who have done quite well up to this course, all of a sudden find that their brain doesn't seem to work very well. Many students and teachers blame this dilemma on the fact that the student is attempting for the first time to do "proofs." The reasoning is that this

One of the math courses that creates a great deal of agony for many students is **GEOMETRY**. It seems that many very bright math students who have done quite well up to this course, all of a sudden find that their brain doesn't seem to work very well.

is a new skill and process and that some students just don't have the ability to think and reason logically.

I have another reason that I think causes students to have a problem with geometry. I think the students are being lured out of their normal visual learning strategy into a auditory strategy because some teachers require that the student MUST memorize the axioms, postulates, and theorems. Since most students attempt to memorize auditorially (by repeating them over and over), they naturally would attempt to memorize axioms, etc in the same way.

> I think the students are being lured out of their normal visual learning strategy into a auditory strategy because some teachers require that the student MUST memorize the axioms, postulates, and theorems.

The consequences of this are many fold. It forces the student to learn something in a very boring, lengthy and tedious manner. It takes the student out of a visual learning mode (and geometry is highly visual). And, many students decide that something is wrong with them and buy into the notion that they "just can't do geometry!"

An alternative way to memorize the axioms, postulates, and theorems is to utilize the "Vocabulary Strategy." For example, there is a postulate in geometry which sounds like the following: **"When two parallel lines are cut by a straight line, corresponding angles are equal."** A visual representation looks like the drawing shown to the right. If a student would

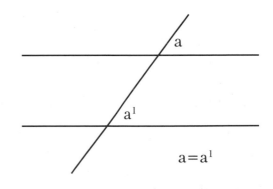

remember the drawing, he could state the postulate by describing the drawing.

How to Write

Some students have a very difficult time writing compositions or term papers. They seem to have the knowledge and information in their heads but can't get it out on paper in an organized fashion. Their papers, therefore, are written in a scattered and hit or miss fashion.

One reason for this is that some students do not know how to "chunk down" the thoughts that are in their head. "Chunking down" is the process of taking general ideas and breaking them down into organized and more specific ideas (some of this is covered in the **Learning Styles** section). This is also what I teach students to do when they learn to visually read — start with the question "What is this about?" and then check to see how the author has broken down the chapter or book.

To assist the students in learning how to do this, I tell them the metaphor or story about how my son, Chris, learned this very important task. I introduce the story by telling them that even though he was a honor student in high school, when he was asked to write a composition, he was terrible. This story totally turned him around in one session. In fact, the next week, he wrote a five paragraph composition that the teacher declared a "model composition!" Since that time through college and into law school, he has been regarded as an excellent writer. He was even a co-editor of the Texas Law Review while he was a student in law school at the University of Texas.

My story begins on the following page:

The Writing Story

"So, Chris, what do you want to write about?"

"I want to write about football, because I like to play it."

"What do you want the purpose or theme of your composition to be about?"

"About how playing football teaches you good work habits, cooperation with others, and discipline."

"O.K., but that's too general and you will have to break it down or subdivide it. Some examples would be: by level of play — little league, junior high, high school, college, and pros; or by the people who are involved — players, coaches, umpires, and fans; or by the way it is played — offense and defense. What ideas do you have?"

"I want to write about high school football because that's what I play."

"O.K., you need to break that down a little more. How do you want to do it?"

"I want to write about the players because I'm a player."

"O.K., how do you want to break that down?"

"I want to break it down into offense and defense, and I want to write about the defense because that's what I play."

"O.K., how will you break that down?"

The defense is composed of the line, linebackers, and the defensive backfield. I want to write about the line because that's what I play."

"O.K., break that down one more time."

"The way we play the defensive line is composed of nose guard, tackles and ends and I want to write about the nose guard position because that's what I play."

"O.K., so your story is about how you learned those things by playing nose guard in the defensive line in high school football? Each of the breakdowns can be a paragraph in your five paragraph composition. Each paragraph will have a topical sentence telling the readers what the paragraph is about, then you will support the topical sentence by your own experiences which relate to that when you played high school football. Do you understand?"

"I see what you mean. Thanks!"

So, when you are starting to write a paper, ask yourself the question "What do I want to write about?" and/or "What is my purpose or reason for writing this?" Then break the topic down into some logical subdivisions and write about each of them or the ones connected to your purpose. Start with a section or paragraph about your purpose. Then follow with the sections about each breakdown, then write a summary describing what the writing was about.

Learning Language Arts

One of the most difficult courses for students to learn visually are language arts courses such as English or a foreign language. I think the primary reason is that it is presented or taught so auditorially. A large percentage of the course is devoted to learning labels for experience rather then learning the experience itself. The purpose for learning Language Arts, either English or a foreign language, is to learn how to communicate with others — both spoken and written and both sending and receiving. Instead, a majority of the teaching time is spent learning the labels so we can talk ABOUT Language Arts rather then do it.

So, we spend an inordinate amount of time learning what an adverb is , what a preposition is, etc., and very little time learning what a preposition or adverb does in the experience of communicating. Effective communication involves the transmission of EXPERIENCE through the use of words or non-verbal communication. Too many times we get so caught up in the study of words that we forget about the experience we are supposed to be communicating.

The communicating of experience is transmission through the senses. So, after the communication, the internal sensory or subjective experience would have information stored in one or more of the senses: visual, auditory, kinesthetic, smell, taste (v,a,k,s,t). If the subjective experience or (v,a,k,s,t) of the recipient is the same as the sender, the communication is successful. The degree to which they are different is the degree of mis-communication.

To attempt to use words to describe full sensory experience is almost futile. It is, however, the primary way we communicate. One of the difficulties lies in the "slippage" in meaning from full sensory experience to words and then in the additional "slippage" when the recipient translates the words into his or her own sensory experience. This is caused by the difference in the meanings (in the form of the sensory experience) we have attached to the words.

The study of language arts, therefore, should be about how the rules of grammar and the parts of speech affect the transmission of experience and not in how to define them. For example, if I am trying to create a full sensory experience in you with my language patterns, what function do nouns play? Verbs? Adverbs? Adjectives? Prepositions?, etc.

> The study of language arts... should be about how the rules of grammar and the parts of speech affect the transmission of experience...

As an example, when you are visually processing my words, how do each of the parts of speech affect your internal images? They do have a different function or impact, do they not? Nouns are the objects in the picture. Verbs dictate how they move. Adjectives spice up the look of the objects. Adverbs spice up the action. Prepositions show relationships of objects to other objects, etc.

So, making vivid pictures of the effect of the part of speech on the sensory experience, makes the study of parts of speech come alive and gives a reason to learn them. This makes more sense then having a bunch of definitions to memorize. It also gives a reason to learn the parts of speech.

Another way some students like to do this is to imagine they were drawing a cartoon strip and think of the different effects the parts of speech would have on the drawing of the cartoon strip. If they drew one without any adjectives or adverbs, how would it look? Kinda dull, right?

We can also investigate how the rules of grammar affect pictures or even the kinesthetic action of an experience. What effect does a period have on the experience? What is the difference in your visual and/or kinesthetic experience in this: I chased the dog down the street. After the rain made puddles, we ran through them. And this: I chased the dog down the street after the rain made puddles, we ran through them. Also, what was the effect on you, visually and kinesthetically, of the comma?

In my experience, students think this way of learning grammar rules and parts of speech is far more interesting and simpler then memorizing definitions. Maybe, if we taught Language Arts more like this, we wouldn't have to repeat it and have English classes year after year.

Foreign Languages

In many foreign language classes, the majority of the time and effort is spent in learning terminology or what words mean. The most common way used by students is the old vocabulary strategy of saying the foreign word and then saying the equivalent English word and then the definition. This is a totally auditory strategy and is boring, tedious and time consuming — and it doesn't work very well.

Since, learning a foreign language is also about communicating experience, I have taught my students to use the Vocabulary Strategy (covered previously) in their foreign language class. For example, if they want to learn the meaning of the foreign word, they create a real life experience of the word and then insert the foreign word into it. They then say the foreign word WHILE looking at the real life experience and then describe the experience in either English or the foreign language. They would insert the English equivalent if they wanted to do translations. This attaches the real life experience to the sight and sound of the foreign word.

TIPS FOR PARENTS AND TEACHERS

Learning Communication Skills

The ability to communicate effectively with students is highly important if we are to be able to help the students learn academic skills and succeed in school. In fact, our inability to communicate our desires and ideas is one of the biggest frustrations of parents and teachers.

Major Principles Of Good Communication

1. **You communicate to get a response**. When you communicate, you do so to get a response from the other person. You may want him to understand, to be motivated, to feel praised, or to feel loved. But you want the response.

2. **The meaning of your communication is the response you get-- regardless of your intention.** All communication has intention. That is the purpose of your communication -- what you are trying to accomplish -- the response you want. Too many times we think the meaning of our communication is based on our intention rather than on the response we get. We attempt to motivate a student to study hard for a test because we want him to do well. Our intention is our concern and desire for the best for the student. However, many times he will rebel against or resist our attempts. The meaning of this communication is resistance or rebellion.

3. **You are responsible for the response you get.** If you are not getting the response you want -- do something else. Resistance is a statement from him to you that you need to do something else to get the response you want. If you persist in doing the same thing over and over and continue to get resistance, that is a statement about your inflexibility as a communicator.

4. Every behavior, no matter how bizarre is grounded in positive intention. A person's behavior is ALWAYS the best choice available to him according to the information he has and his model of the world. This is a very important principle. If you can assume or find positive intention in those around you, then there is no need for them to resist you. You can not only assume positive intention, you can actively search for it. You may even ask them "What is the positive intention behind that behavior?" or "What does that behavior do for you?"

5. Good communicators will communicate TO the other persons model of the world and positive intention -- not FROM their own intention and model of the world. They will pace the other person's model of the world and positive intention and then lead them to the response he wants. So many times we assume that others think as we do and we communicate with them based on that assumption. It is VERY important to find out where they are coming from and to accept and appreciate their model of the world and positive intention. Once you get this message across that you accept and appreciate them for who they uniquely are, they are receptive to receive your message.

6. You can't do any of the above without rapport. Rapport is the ability to get others to want to listen to what you have to say -- to respect and even trust that what you are communicating to them is important to them.

Rapport is the ability to get others to want to listen to what you have to say...

If you don't have rapport with another person, your important message **WILL NOT GET THROUGH**.

Rapport is the

Basic Prerequisite

of Effective

Communication.

Finding Positive Intention

Probably one of the most powerful and useful communication ideas, but especially for parents and teachers, is the notion of looking for and finding positive intention behind all behaviors. Even behaviors which seem bizarre, crazy, wrong, or even hurtful. Yes, I am talking about when your son or daughter does any of the following; throws a temper tantrum, is rebellious, doesn't mind you, hits his brother or sister, does poorly in school, gets in trouble in school, doesn't do homework, smokes, or does drugs. All of these examples of negative behaviors have positive intention. In fact, it's the positive intention which drives the behavior. And, the negative behavior won't change until the positive intention is recognized, accepted as valid, and satisfied. So, it is extremely important to separate behavior from intention and then to make sure that the intention is positive.

> **It's the positive intention which drives the behavior. And, the negative behavior won't change until the positive intention is recognized, accepted as valid, and satisfied.**

But first let's describe what positive intention is. Your intention behind a behavior or communication is what you want to do or accomplish. It's your purpose for doing the behavior. It's your reason. Many times you have multiple intentions at different logical levels. In fact, they are sometimes embedded in each other in a kind of hierarchy. Most of the time, many of the intentions are out of conscious awareness. Some of them come from our past and we have forgotten about them and where they came from. Some of them are pretty obvious. The obvious ones usually get dealt with very rapidly. The negative behaviors with hidden, unconscious positive intention are the ones that cause the chronic problems.

So a part of the skill we need is to be able to elicit the hidden, unconscious positive intention. But before we learn that skill, we have to understand the notion of positive intention. The second part of the skill is to be able to satisfy the positive intention when we find it.

The power of finding positive intention is in the response it elicits from the other person. If you blame, act judgmental, criticize, or otherwise attach a negative intention to the behavior or communication, you will automatically get a defensive response, or he will withdraw, or he will counter-attack. You become the enemy. If you are honestly and actively assuming positive intention and looking for it, there is no need for the other person to defend himself against you or to attack you. You are not a threat, you are an ally.

> The power of finding positive intention is in the response it elicits from the other person.

When I first work with a student who is having trouble in school, I assume that the reason he is having trouble is because his learning strategies don't work well. I also assume that if he had a easy, quick, and fun way to learn that he would jump at it. I talk to him as if all the above is true. I tell him that it is not his fault that he doesn't know how to learn. I tell him that the school system presupposed that he knew how and never got around to teaching him how to learn in the classroom. I then proceed to check out his learning strategies and to teach him better ones.

Even though the student described above may be flunking, about to be kicked out of school, is a behavior problem in school or home, or is a surly, angry teenager, I treat him in that way. So, what are the positive intentions built in to my assumptions? They are: he would learn if he knew how, once I teach him a better way he will change his behavior, there is nothing wrong with him, and he is an OK person.

If I teach a student how to learn in ways that work, and he still doesn't do well in school, I assume that he has something hampering him at a different logical level. I then look for his highly valued criteria or values or limiting beliefs. If over the years, the student has been presented with lots of evidence that he is dumb or can't do schoolwork successfully, he may have started to believe it. If he now has the capability to do better but believes that he is dumb, he won't use the learning strategies. It is important at that point to change the limiting belief.

...by getting an answer to the question, "What does this behavior do for me?" Or, "How does this behavior benefit me?" Or, "What am I wanting to happen when I do this behavior?"

So, how do we find hidden, unconscious positive intention? You can either put yourself in the other person's experience and guess the positive intention by getting an answer to the question "What does this behavior do for me?" Or, "How does this behavior benefit me?" Or, "What am I wanting to happen when I do this behavior?" Remember to look for POSITIVE reasons.

You can also directly ask the other person any of the above questions. It is EXTREMELY important that you do it with rapport, bolstered by a caring, accepting, curious tone and demeanor. That's why it is so important that you believe in the notion of positive intention. If you don't believe they had positive intention, your non-verbals will give you away and you will come across as incongruent.

When you get an answer to one of the above questions, you can elicit more important embedded intentions by taking the answer you got and asking the same questions about it, "And what does that do for you?" You can elicit a chain of embedded intentions, each more powerful then the one before, by continuing to ask the question of each answer you get. When you have an idea of what the positive intention is, check it out with them by asking the question "So, what you were really wanting with that behavior was _____?"

Once you know what the positive intention is, particularly the more important ones, talk to him as though it were true. Applaud and appreciate the fact that he is trying to do something positive and offer to assist him in achieving his positive intention. Comment on the fact that the positive intention is more consistent with the kind of person he is than is the negative behavior. Help him come up with a new behavior that is consistent with the kind of person he is AND which will satisfy his positive intention.

> Once you know what the positive intention is, particularly the more important ones, talk to him as though it were true. Applaud and appreciate the fact that he is trying to do something positive and offer to assist him in achieving his positive intention.

The more you practice this technique, the more skilled and smooth you will become in asking the questions and listening for the response and in finding the positive intention. In my experience, as you do this more and more, you will find that other people treat you significantly better AND you treat others better.

Getting Rapport With Mirroring

One of the major principles of communication is the notion that we will not be able to get our message across to another person if we do not have rapport with him. Here we will explore the ways to quickly get rapport with anyone.

There are many ways to get rapport and one of the best is to mirror the other person's unconscious verbal and nonverbal behaviors. It is best to do this smoothly and without being obvious. You do this by incorporating the mirroring into your natural responses in the conversation. The more important behaviors you can mirror are as follows:

There are many ways to get rapport and one of the best is to mirror the other person's unconscious verbal and nonverbal behaviors.

Facial Expression: There are people with stoic faces and people with very animated faces. People will move their eyebrows, smile, frown, nod their head, etc., as they talk -- or not. Your task is to mimic or mirror their facial expression as closely as possible. If they are stoic, you will want to be stoic.

Eye Contact: There is a myth which says that you must maintain constant eye contact with other people. With some people, however, this type of eye contact is disturbing. So, how do you know what to do? You mirror the type of eye contact the other people give you. If they hold eye contact for long periods of time, so do you. If they look away periodically, so do you **AND** you look at the same location for the same duration of time and with the same tempo.

Arm Position: If they fold their arms, you fold your arms the same way. If they lean on one arm on a table, you lean on one arm on the table -- if you can.

Body Lean: If they lean forward, you lean forward. If they lean back in the chair, you lean back.

Leg Position: Notice how their legs are crossed or if they are not crossed. If they cross their legs at the ankle, you cross your legs at the ankle. If they cross their legs at the knee, you cross your legs at the knee. One word of caution for ladies; if you are wearing a short skirt and you are mirroring a man, you may not want to mirror his leg position -- just skip this one.

Gestures: The type and tempo of gestures are very important to mirror. If they have choppy gestures, you **RESPOND** to with the same type of choppy gestures. Other types of gestures you will want to notice and mirror are; powerful, smooth, flowing, or no gestures.

Height: As much as possible, do not stand over somebody sitting or standing close to you. This is especially important with children. Get down to their eye level even if it means getting down on one knee. Also with people sitting in chairs, like wheel chairs, do not stand close to them while they remain seated. Lean over or somehow get down to their eye level.

All of these mirroring techniques should be done smoothly and elegantly **AND** while responding to their conversation. If they shift their position, it is okay to wait until some natural break in the conversation to mirror the new position. You can do it while you ask a question or while you are commenting on what they just said.

After you have practiced these new skills and have become smooth in their use, you will notice a different response in the people around you. You may even notice a different response in yourself to the people around you.

Getting Rapport With Your Voice

How do you build auditory rapport? This is just one more communication technique which can be used by anyone. Rapport is a necessary prerequisite to effective communication, whether with children, business colleagues, clients, customers, friends or enemies. Auditory rapport is particularly useful for those who use the telephone. You basically get rapport by mirroring the voice patterns of other persons. Some of the voice patterns to mirror (or mimic) are as follows:

Timbre: Do they have a special or unique quality in their voice that is connected to an internal state -- like playfulness, seriousness, excitement, etc? You will want to mirror this very gradually if their timbre is very different then yours. Examples of when this is useful are when you are talking to a child, or when the other person has a playful quality in his voice, or the opposite -- when he is very somber or serious.

Tempo: How fast or slow are they talking? This is very important. There are individuals who very carefully and slowly pick their words and there are individuals who can talk very rapidly -- and for the most part they do not trust each other or have rapport because of this very quality. One of them has to adjust the tempo of his voice if quality communication has even a chance.

Pitch: How high or low are they talking? Obviously, if a soprano is talking to a bass, they cannot match each other exactly. If you will move up or down in your pitch range to a level that is comfortable and toward the other persons pitch, it will positively affect rapport.

Projection: How forceful are they talking? This can be thought of as the volume of air they are expelling when they talk. This is also one of the very important qualities. If they are forceful, you need to mirror that in your verbal response to them. If they are soft spoken, you mirror that quality.

Breathing: Are they breathing? If so, where? In the top of the chest, mid-chest, or lower chest? Also, how fast are they breathing? Are they breathing in short, rapid breaths? Or, do they have even and moderated breathing? Or, do they take deep breaths and slowly exhale? Whichever of these they do, you mirror or match it. If you can breathe as they breathe, you can more easily match their tempo and force.

Rhythm: Is there a beat or cadence in their voice? Do they have pauses or is it a monotone? Where do they breathe and does the breath come in a regular or irregular rhythm? Whatever their rhythm, you mirror it as best as you can.

Emphasis: What words do they hit hard or hang on to? Which words do they *d-r-a-w* out or **SAY FORCEFULLY**. Whichever words they do this with, you mirror them in your response by using the same word with the same emphasis.

Modal Operators: Which of the following types of words do they use?

Necessity: need, must, got to, should, have to, will (or the negative as in must not, should not, will not, etc.)

Possibility: want to, choose, able, can, ability (or the negative as in don't want, cannot, not able to, etc.)

   Contingency: wish, might, maybe, would, could, try, perhaps, might not, would not, etc.

As before, choose the same modal operators they choose and incorporate them in your response. Of course all of these mirroring techniques should be done gracefully and smoothly and built in to your natural response to the other person. If you are obvious and awkward, you may lose rapport.

Another way to get rapport auditorially is to match the way they process information. When we think, we process our experiences and information in one or more of our senses. We can visually process by making pictures in our head. We can auditorially process by talking to ourselves and internally repeating conversations or other sounds. We can kinesthetically process by accessing emotions or body sensations.

If a person is visually processing, it will help communication if you will help him paint a picture in his mind. It will also help if you will use sensory based words or predicates that are visual in nature. A few of the many visual predicates are; see, look, picture, clear, vision, light, shine, reveal, image, view, appear, show, watch, and focus. One of the ways you will know he is visually processing is by listening to the visual predicates he uses. You simply match his visual predicates in your response.

If a person is auditorially processing, you will hear him use auditory predicates such as; hear, say, talk, discuss, praise, call, noise, argue, quiet, speak, listen, tone, and sound. These are just a few of the many choices of auditory predicates. To strengthen rapport, you simply match his auditory predicates in your response.

Kinesthetic processors use predicates such as; feel, tough, solid, unbalanced, warm, rough, tension, connect, smooth, firm, twist, touch, and soft -- to name just a few. Again, you simply match the types of predicates he uses in order to gain rapport.

Another way to determine how others are processing information and experience is to watch their eye accessing cues. When they look, with unfocused eyes, to one of the six locations as indicated in the figure below, they will be accessing visually, auditorially, or kinesthetic as indicated.

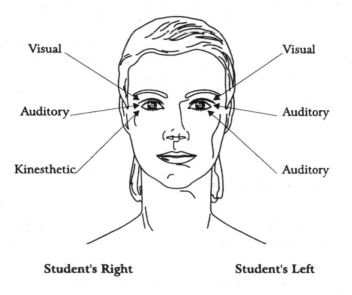

Student's Right   **Student's Left**

When you see them look up to their left or right, you use visual predicates to match their eye accessing cues. When they look straight to their left or right or down to their left, you use auditory predicates in your response to them. If they look down to the right, you use kinesthetic predicates.

This pattern of eye accessing is true for a large percentage of the population. Left handed individuals will sometimes reverse the pattern from left to right. People with mixed dominance may have their own unique eye accessing pattern. You can ask them specially designed questions to determine their unique pattern.

Learning to Visualize

Sometimes I will have students who swear that they cannot make internal images. They claim they have no pictures at all. When this happens, I stop the normal academic learning until I can teach them to visualize.

Many times these students simply are not aware of the internal images they have. In order to build this awareness, I may ask them to describe their pet, or a favorite TV show or movie, or their favorite movie star. This gets them into the state of making pictures in their head. I then start assisting them in noticing that they make these descriptions off of their internal images.

Another way I build awareness is to ask them to think of a family member or a friend. I then ask them "If a friend were to silently enter the room, would you recognize him?" Of course, the answer is "yes." I tell them at that point that they cannot do that unless they have an internal picture of what the person looks like. I then gently assist them in becoming aware of the internal image.

"If a friend were to silently enter the room, would you recognize him?"

Another way is to set an imaginary table in front of them -- complete with glass, fork, spoon, knife, and plate with different kinds of food on it. I set the table while they watch. I show and tell them what the food items are and where they are placed on the plate. I then ask them to drink from the glass, eat a particular item with the fork, or other common eating action. They cannot successfully do this unless they maintain an image of the table setting.

Another reason some students think they cannot make internal pictures is that the internal pictures they do have are not as clear as their external visual experience or they are different in other ways. For example, they may not be in color, or they are still pictures, or they are foggy or blurred, or they may move too fast. They, therefore, discount and consciously ignore their internal pictures. They unconsciously process visual information, but not consciously. With these students, pointing out the types of internal visual experience they have and helping them strengthen them is all that is required.

Also, some students need to shut their eyes in order to become aware of their internal images. Many times such students will be confused and unable to do some of the tasks I ask of them. When I notice that they are trying to do the task with their eyes open, I ask them to attempt it with their eyes closed. In many instances, this simple adjustment is all that is needed.

One way to help a struggling student strengthen the picture is to have him write out the word on a chalkboard or sheet of paper. As he holds the word up in front of his face, have him stare at it while slowly closing his eyes. Instruct him to hold the image of the word as his eyes close. This may have to be repeated several times. Sometimes it is helpful to have the word written out in the student's favorite color.

Another helpful technique is to have the student imagine he is writing the word in the air while looking at the word. After a few attempts, hide the word and have him trace the word in the air with his finger identical to what he thinks the word looks like. After doing this enough times so that the student is comfortable with it, change the major muscle tracing movements to micro muscle movements that he can do without drawing attention to himself.

As the awareness of the internal pictures becomes stronger, I then start giving the students tasks designed to strengthen their ability to make pictures AND to start to trust their pictures. One of the best ways to do this is to get each of them to make a picture of a simple word THEY ALREADY KNOW HOW TO

SPELL. I then ask them to spell the word backwards (from right to left). As they successfully do this, I ask them to do it with longer and longer words. I then have them try with words they don't know how to spell (I tell them to take a picture of the word with their mind's eye and remember what the word looks like, then spell it backwards).

After they can successfully do this, I move them on to telephone numbers, social security numbers, math formulas, etc. By this time, their confidence levels are pretty high.

At this point, I get them to develop the first stages of photographic memory by having them look at something (a word on a billboard or sign, or a title of a book, or an address, etc) and take a picture of it, then look away and notice they can retain the image. I will then have them describe the picture in detail or spell the image backwards to strengthen the retention of the image. After they can do this, I have them move on to phrases, sentences, charts, diagrams, formulas, etc. At this point, they don't have to spell things backwards, they simply remember and trust the whole picture they took.

Building Self-Esteem

Self esteem or self image comes in answer to the question "What kind of person am I?" The answers to the question are in terms of attributes or qualities we assign to ourselves or allow to be assigned to us (e.g. kind, loving, bright, hard worker, lazy, tough, independent.). These attributes are usually assigned based on behavior (or lack of) and sometimes on intention; so, a general formula for helping your child build his self esteem is to:

> 1) Notice a good behavior.
> 2) Think up an attribute it demonstrates.
>
> And then 3) Comment on that connection to the child.

You can do this as the behaviors naturally occur or you can systematically build your child's self esteem by deliberately thinking up behaviors they regularly do and by preparing yourself for when the behaviors occur. You do this in the following manner:

1. Identify something they have done well and will probably do again. It will help if they are pleased about it.

2. Ask yourself, "Of what positive attribute or quality is this a demonstration?" or "What kind of person would be pleased by this behavior?

3. When the behavior occurs, make comments to him or her like, "That lets me know that you are a very (name the attribute) person!" or "That demonstrates that you are the kind of person that is very (name the attribute)!"

As an example, suppose your child is very touched and sensitive to the family pet who has a thorn in its paw and may be trying to soothe the pet. You could comment "That lets me know you are a very sensitive and caring person" or "That's how a loving person acts."

You can also identify routine or important negative behaviors that they DON'T do and make comments on the kind of person who does not engage in these behaviors.

You can also identify routine or important negative behaviors that they DON'T do and make comments on the kind of person who does not engage in these behaviors. Examples are those children who do not; do drugs, leave messes, misbehave, hurt others, etc. If your child behaves "poorly" or in an "unacceptable" manner, find the positive intention behind the behavior and make sure your comment has in it a positive attribute related to "the (name the attribute) kind of person who would have these intentions!"

Another way to do this is to decide if the behavior was caused by an extra-ordinary and/or unexpected occurrence or was it a "mistake" on his part. If it was unexpected, find the positive intention based upon what they "thought" was happening. Identify the positive attribute and the positive intention behind that. Give this feedback in the same manner as before.

If he knew it was going to happen or if it happens repeatedly, challenge the negative behavior as NOT a demonstration of the kind of person he really is. Label the incident a mistake. Help him identify a new and more appropriate behavior **WHICH WOULD BE A DEMONSTRATION OF THE KIND OF PERSON HE WANTS TO BE!** Have him mentally practice the new behavior several times in possible future incidents so he will automatically behave in the manner he wants. Identify the positive intention behind the new behavior and assign an attribute to it. Give him this feedback in the same manner as before.

Remembering Names

Remembering the names of people is an important skill that greatly aids the communication process. Using the other person's name when you greet him is impressive to many people and allows rapport to build more quickly. I will share with you a very easy strategy for remembering names. If you will practice this strategy several times, it will soon become automatic.

1. When you initially greet someone and he tells you his name, visualize the name being printed on his forehead or right below his chin. If he has an unusual name or a name with multiple possible spellings, ask him to spell it for you. This will give you the opportunity and time to spell it out more clearly in your mind's eye. This step attaches the image of the name to how he looks. If you talk to him on the telephone and do not know how he looks, attach the sight of the name to the sound of his voice saying your name or his normal greeting to you.

2. While you look at his face with the image of his name printed on it, say his name as many times as is socially acceptable. Be sure you say his name WHILE you are looking at his face and name. This attaches the sound of his name to how he looks.

3. While continuing to look at his face and the image of his name and while using his name, find some association of which his name reminds you. Picture that association in the background or foreground of the same image you have built in your mind. So, if his first name reminds you of somebody else with that same name, put an image of that person behind or beside him. If his last name reminds you of a place, change the background of the picture to include that place. This kinesthetically and visually attaches the association to how he looks and the sound of his name.

4. If you will practice his name this way four to six times, you will remember it. If you want to remember it for a longer time, you have to periodically bring up the images and practice the connections over a longer period of time. This practice drops the name into long term memory. The longer you practice it, the longer you will remember it.

The reason most people don't remember names is that they do not take the time and energy to store the name in their brain. Most of us are thinking about how we look, or what we are going to say, or we are wondering what the other persons think about us. Their names just kind of goes in one ear and out the other and never registers.

Many people will lament, "I can remember faces but names escape me!" That indicates that they can remember what they see but the sound of the name never registers. This strategy installs the name visually, auditorially, and kinesthetically. It also installs the association in all three senses.

Many people will attempt only associations and then get crossed up because they don't have a back-up in another sense. They may attempt to remember Mr. Rocky's name by associating it with the Rocky Mountains. A few days later, however, they meet Mr. Rocky and call him Mr. Alps or Mr. Everest or Mr. Mountain.

Most of the steps outlined above can be carried out while you are engaging the other person in light "get to know you" conversation. Questions about the origin or spelling of the name are actually a compliment to the other person because you care enough to get his name correct. In addition, after you have practiced this strategy a few times, it will tend to become an automatic habit -- like most successful skills.

Changing Limiting Beliefs in Students

Many times when students struggle in school they take it personally which means they think it means something about them as a person. They think it means they are stupid or that they can't learn or that they are not a good student, etc. Many of these beliefs adversely affect their self esteem and performance. Most of the time, in my experience, struggling in school simply means that the skills the student is attempting to use to learn the material do not work very well.

The student doesn't know that he or she is supposed to do something different. They don't know there is anything different to do, so the diligent ones keep doing what they think they are supposed to do -- some of the other students get bored or frustrated and quit trying -- some become behavior problems in school and home -- some drop out of school -- some turn to gangs and/or drugs.

Much of this handbook has been about different academic skills that students need in order to do better in school. We have covered such academic skills as learning: new spelling words, math facts, vocabulary words, how to read with comprehension, how to make any subject interesting, how to remember to do things, etc. These academic skills are very important and the lack of these skills is the biggest deterrent to succeeding in school.

The belief that many students have, however, regarding their inability to learn is another big deterrent to succeeding in school. If they believe they can't learn or do well in school, then they have difficulty even trying the new academic skills. Changing their belief from "I can't learn" to "I can learn" is very important and very empowering.

The structure of changing beliefs is as follows:

1. They start to attend to counter-examples of the old belief which they cannot refute.

2. This gets them to start to doubt the old belief.

3. They find enough counter-examples to finally disbelieve the former belief.

4. They start to open up to the prospect of a new way of thinking about the old experience.

5. They start to believe the new belief.

6. The new belief solidifies.

One way to utilize the above to change their beliefs in school is as follows:

1. Reframe their past failures as mistakes rather then a statement about their ability. Tell them that they simply have not learned some of the simple skills that other students have learned. ...And, it's not their fault -- nobody taught them! We presupposed that they knew how to study and learn -- and we were wrong.

> ...And, it's not their fault -- nobody taught them! We presupposed that they knew how to study and learn -- and we were wrong.

2. Give them some demonstrations of some of the new skills. Picturing a word and spelling it from right to left is a excellent demonstration. I tell them if they can do that then I know they have the basic ability to be successful in

school. Also, showing them the difference when they are reading successfully and reading unsuccessfully is a good demonstration.

3. As they perform some of the new skills, repeat the reframe in step 1 and say "Now that you are learning these skills, you can become a good student too. In the past you struggled in school, not because you didn't have the ability but because you didn't know what to do differently. Now you know how to do it in a way that works really well. So now you can succeed in school in the future."

> "Now that you are learning these skills, you can become a good student, too. In the past you struggled in school, not because you didn't have the ability but because you didn't know what to do differently. Now you know how to do it in a way that works really well -- so now you can succeed in school in the future."

4. Every time they have a new success, connect the evidence of success with statements similar to the statement in step 3 to reassure them that now their school experiences are indeed different. Treat them as being different. Raise your expectations to a slightly higher level and than when they meet those expectations, repeat the statement again. Continue to reinforce the new belief that **THEY CAN LEARN**. The continued reinforcement connected to irrefutable evidence of success will cause them to change their old beliefs to something more useful in school.

Turning Kids On To School or How to Affect Attitude

Have you ever had the experience of somebody saying something to you and all of a sudden your whole perspective shifted. Suddenly, you thought differently about the subject. Your outlook, your feelings, and ultimately your behaviors related to the subject started to change.

All the way through my public school and college (until my junior year in college), I only wanted to be an average student. I wanted to hide in the crowd. I definitely did not want to "stand out" and be in the limelight. Flunking would attract attention, too. To just be "one of the guys", to be "well-liked", and to just "get along" was my primary motivation in school. As you can well imagine, my grades reflected this attitude. Oh, every now and then, I would get a B and even rarely and miraculously on some easy course I would luck into an A. Sometimes, curses of curses, I would slip into a D and once I got a F (disaster!). Usually though, my grades were Cs.

When I was a second semester junior in college, however, my roommate (who was a straight A student) inadvertently said something to me over lunch one day that instantly shifted my whole perspective on school and learning. From that day on, I thought about school and learning differently. But more importantly, I no longer wanted to be average in school or out of school. From that day on I wanted to excel, to be one of a kind, to lead. What a gift my roommate gave me and it has stayed with me to this day.

> ...my roommate (who was a straight A student) inadvertently said something to me over lunch one day that instantly shifted my whole perspective on school and learning. From that day on, I thought about school and learning differently.

Please understand, I didn't instantly become a straight A student (although I did get on the Dean's Honor Roll) nor did I become a leader in campus politics. This is primarily because **I did not know how to excel in school.** I had to learn how to study differently, to take tests differently, to listen in class differently, to do homework differently, and to build my confidence and self-esteem. Unfortunately, I had to learn these things myself and it took a while. But a miracle still had occurred over that lunch.

So, how do these types of phenomenon occur. Are they magical and/or acts of God, not to be duplicated by us mere mortals? I hope you will agree with me that these are "wonderful" moments in our history. We can look back and say "that was a turning point in my life!" Wouldn't it be nice to be able to replicate this phenomenon with struggling students intentionally and by conscious design? If your answer is <u>yes</u>, read on.

> So, how do these types of phenomenon occur. Are they magical and/or acts of God, not to be duplicated by us mere mortals?

Highly Valued Criteria

Human beings are constantly in the process of sorting through what is important to them in their life quest and what is not important. These become the standards or criteria by which they guide their life and behaviors. Some of these criteria prove more and more important over the years and become higher valued criteria. A whole hierarchy of these criteria develops over the years, out of conscious awareness, and becomes their perceptual filter for what they believe to be reality and/or what is important. These different perceptual filters, from one person to another, are what cause us to respond differently to the same stimuli or in the same situation. This is why some are turned on to school and learning, for example, while others aren't.

Quite simply, a person turns onto school and learning when something happens to allow him to perceive that school or learning <u>can and will</u> satisfy his highly valued criteria. It is the classic "eureka" or "aha" response. The question to ask now is, "Is it possible to do this intentionally?"

Quite simply, a person turns onto school and learning when something happens to allow him to perceive that school or learning <u>can and will</u> satisfy his highly valued criteria. It is the classic "**eureka**" or "**aha**" response.

The answer is yes! I have studied the structure of this occurrence and the process by which it occurs and can design it rather then wait for it to accidentally occur. In order to consciously design this occurrence with another person, you need two major pieces of information and the skill to use them appropriately.

The two pieces of information are:

1. Know what you want to turn them on to, and

2. Find out their highly valued criteria.

As an example, I was introduced to a ninth grade student whose parents were complaining that he made Cs, Ds, and Fs. He was a bright boy, they claimed, who did well on tests but poorly in homework. He did not seem to be interested in improving himself or doing better in school. This was a pattern from earlier years but his parents were alarmed now because, as a ninth grader, his grades were now going to become a part of his permanent record and affect where he could go to college and chances for a scholarship. Upon further inquiry, I found that the parents were talking about an athletic scholarship rather than academic.

It seems the student was a budding golf pro who had the potential to be great but he had to do well in school so that he could go to the proper college to get his proper golf education. Needless to say, the young man just wanted to turn pro now and not worry about school.

Now as far as I'm concerned, anytime I find a student turned off of school but turned on to sports or a hobby, I know how to find his highly valued criteria. This is called an isomorphic activity to school because they both involve matching elements and relationships. They both involve learning, homework/practice, cooperation, discipline, performance, listening, and other growth skills.

> ...anytime I find a student turned off of school but turned on to sports or a hobby, I know how to find his highly valued criteria.

After talking to the young man for awhile, I found out he liked school in general but disliked homework in particular. He thought homework was "boring and a waste of my time!" I asked him how he did his homework and he said "I go to my room, close the door and try to study." He didn't even play any music.

> **He thought homework was, "boring and a waste of my time!"**

I then asked him if he practiced golf and he and his parents declared he was disciplined and consistent at practicing golf. I next asked him how he practiced golf and he said he and several of his friends would gather at the practice range and practice together. They would laugh and joke with each other but would also try to outdo each other in a friendly way but <u>most</u> importantly critique each other's shots and praise each other's good shots. I asked him what he liked about practice and he said, "It's fun and I'm always improving and getting better and better!"

The burning question I was internally asking myself was, "How does he not see that school and homework provide him with an arena to improve and to get better? How can I help him make that connection?" The answer was obvious. I asked the parents to make arrangements to have the young man study with his friends and to have them ask each other questions about the lessons and to good naturedly coach, critique, and praise each other on their path to improving and getting better in school. (His parents later said that this worked very well but it was hard to arrange it consistently since he did not yet drive.)

I decided to see if I could turn him on to studying by himself. As before, the answer was in his golf game. To the question "Do you ever practice golf by yourself when friends aren't available?" He responded "Yes." "How do you do it," I asked? "And is it enjoyable?" He replied, "I go out on the course and play and I will hit 5 or 6 balls from the same spot." The question I now needed an answer to was "How do you keep that from being repetitive and boring?" His reply "On every shot I try to improve and hit it better than the previous shots."

So in effect, when he did his homework, he would notice how each problem was like the previous problems and get bored by the repetitiveness and sameness. In golf, he would get into his competitive nature and make it different by <u>doing it better each time!</u> At this point, transferring the skill from golf to homework was a simple task.

How to Elicit Criteria

A major presupposition behind eliciting criteria is the following: When highly valued criteria are met or violated by situations, happenings, or behaviors in a person's world, he will react with an emotional response. The emotional response will be positive (i.e., happy, excited, pleased, ecstatic, etc.) when criteria are met and negative (i.e., mad, irritated, frustrated, disgusted, etc.) when criteria are violated or not met. So in essence, a negative or positive emotional experience allows us an opportunity to elicit criteria. The more emotional the response, the more highly valued the criteria.

The criteria is revealed in the answer to the question, **"What is it about the experience that causes you to feel the way you do?"** So, for example, in the previous story of the golfer, when he was asked what he liked about playing golf, he responded, "I like to improve my game and get better and better." When he was asked what he didn't like about school he answered, "Homework -- it's dull and boring and a waste of my time. The problems are all the same."

> So in essence, a negative or positive emotional experience allows us an opportunity to elicit criteria. The more emotional the response, the more highly valued the criteria.

So, in essence, any emotional response in a person offers the opportunity to elicit criteria. A strategy for doing this is to get answers to the following questions:

1. How do you feel about _____ ? (_____ is whatever caused the emotions) and
2. What is it **about** _____ that is so important to you?

As they elaborate on the answers to question #2, you listen for criteria. In fact, usually they will respond to the questions with multiple criteria. If you will keep asking the questions you can get multiple criteria. Also, a way to get more criteria of a higher value is to ask question 2 of each criterion you elicit. This will give you a hierarchy of highly valued criteria which means you can now "stack" multiple criteria into one sentence when you are trying to turn them on to something.

How to Turn Them ON

The first thing you want to know now that you are about to attempt to turn them on to school is -- are they turned off of school totally or just some aspect of school? Or, are they just not turned on to school? Sometimes students have simply never made the connection with **how** school can help them achieve their highly valued criteria. Other students may be so turned off of one particular aspect of school that it contaminates their whole attitude. An example of the latter was the golfer previously mentioned who didn't like homework because it was dull and boring.

> Sometimes students have simply never made the connection with **how** school can help them achieve their highly valued criteria.

Regardless of which case you have, your immediate task is to find some logical way to convince them that school or the dissatisfying aspect of school can help them get what they want -- to have their highly valued criteria satisfied. You have two choices, you can either free-wheel it and dream up logical connections or you can find out how the student does it in other like-type contexts.

If you decide the former, your strategy is to dream up logical connections and then to try them out on the student. You keep trying different possibilities until you get a positive response. Once you get the initial response, you and/or the student can elaborate on the possibilities in order to build intensity and strengthen the connection. A more precise way is the latter way. Find in the student a context or situation that the student is turned on to which is isomorphic to school or the distasteful task. How to make the connection can be precisely found in the isomorphic context. An isomorphism, by the way, exists when you have two different contexts (e.g. sports and school) with matching elements and relationships (e.g., practice/homework affects performance/grades).

As stated previously, sports and hobbies are excellent isomorphic possibilities. Favorite subjects in school, learning to drive a car, ride a bike, or roller skate are other good examples.

Once you have selected an appropriate isomorphic activity to which the student is turned on, you start asking questions to determine where the isomorphism breaks down (e.g. the golfer liked to practice golf but did not like homework). Once you have found the breakdown, you start eliciting the difference in criteria <u>and/or</u> the difference in the way the student is thinking about the two. Once you've determined these differences, you have a precise blueprint as to how to turn on the student.

> Once you've determined these differences, you have a precise blueprint as to how to turn on the student.

Several examples are in order at this point. The first is an example of how this process can occur in the most casual of settings. It occurred with my secretary in my reception room as I was preparing to leave to go exercise.

She remarked, *"I don't see how you can go exercise every day. I wish I could do that! I'm so lazy!"*
"What stops you from doing it?" I curiously asked.
"It's so boring! I know it's supposed to make me healthier and I know I'll regret not doing it when I get older. I just can't get myself to do it --I don't know why."
"What's boring about it?" I asked.

"It's the same thing over and over and you have to work at it -- and sweat." she laughed.

"But Sally," I exclaimed, "you told me the other day that you cleaned your house <u>every</u> Saturday from top to bottom. You said it would pass the white glove test. How is it that you can work at that task over and over and not get bored?"

"Well that's different" she exalted, *"when you get through cleaning house you can see what you've done and you can feel good about how it looks. I really like for my house to be <u>clean</u>!"*

"I think I know what the difference is in the way we think about exercise," I stated. "In fact, this is probably the <u>big</u> difference as to why I <u>want</u> to do it every day and you don't. When I am exercising or even when I'm thinking about going, I'm not thinking about long term health goals or how much I am sweating . I'm thinking about how good I will look and feel when I get through <u>that</u> day. I'm thinking about how good I'm going to feel and look as I walk out of the spa and go back to my office. Also, how good my clothes will look on me. I think about not only how good my body feels but I like to see the progress and accomplishment! Haven't you ever noticed how much better you look physically <u>and</u> how much better you feel emotionally right after the exercise?" I asked.

"You know," she exclaimed, *"you're right. I've never thought about it like that before!"*

So the isomorphism, which I knew about from prior conversations with her, was her compulsion to clean her house on a regular basis and love doing it. The difference in how she thought about that task and not think of it as boring compared to exercise that was boring, was my immediate objective. The primary difference was in terms of feeling good, health wise in the distant future and in feeling good physically and emotionally immediately. Simply put, short-term gratification and immediate results that she could **SEE** turned her on. I just focused her attention on those types of aspects naturally occurring in exercise that she had been ignoring.

Another example, in which I didn't have prior knowledge of the case, was in a workshop called *Turning Kids On To School* I was conducting for a group of teachers. Toward the conclusion of the workshop, one of the teachers went out of the room and brought back a ten year old boy. She raised her hand and asked me to demonstrate the techniques on her son. As she talked, I noticed the other teachers whispering and nodding their heads so I concluded that this youngster had a reputation -- and it wasn't scholarly!

So, picture this: we were standing in front of about 60 teachers, some he knew -- most he did not. He didn't know me but had been listening to the workshop from a room just outside the door. This is not the best type of situation to work with with anybody -- particularly somebody who has been having trouble in school. I started trying to get to know the young man by talking to him about his hobbies and other things he did for fun.

The following interaction ensued:

I asked him if he enjoyed school. His adamant reply was, *"No, I don't like school and nobody is going to convince me that I want to go to school!"*
I agreed with him that task would probably be tough and asked him if he participated in any sports.
"No, I don't like sports, I don't like football, I don't like baseball, and I don't like soccer!"
I asked him if he knew how to ride a bicycle and he replied that he did. I   then asked if he enjoyed riding his bicycle and he said he did. "What is it   about riding your bike that you enjoy?" I asked.
"I can beat my brother!" he said proudly.
"Really! What are you doing when you beat your brother?" I curiously asked.
"We race and jump our bikes off of high things. I can go faster and jump higher t h e n he can!" he proudly exclaimed.
I asked him if his brother was younger then he was and he proclaimed, *"No,*

he is older than I am and I can **B-E-A-T** *him!"*
It was becoming very evident to me and to the teachers that beating his brother was very important to him. So I asked the student, "Well, it sounds like you like to be number one and beat your brother. Do you like to win at other things and beat other people too?"
His reply, *"I like to beat others when I know I'm going to win. I don't like to lose!"*
At that moment I stopped and said to the young man, "Let me talk to the teachers for a minute -- you can listen if you want."

I asked the teachers if they had heard any criteria in our discussion. Some of the criteria the teachers fed back to me were: he's competitive; he likes to win; he wants to beat others; he doesn't want to lose; he likes to be number one.

I agreed with them and replied, more for the young man's ear then the teachers, "Well, what's really amazing to me is that he hasn't figured out yet that the classroom gives him lots of opportunity to win and beat others. In fact he probably hasn't realized yet that he's getting beat every day in there. Of course, I don't know if he <u>can</u> be good enough to beat other students in school. If he is good enough, the classroom can provide him with ample opportunity to feel just as good in school as he does when he beats his brother."

I was watching the young man out of the corner of my eye and could tell he was listening intently. I asked the teachers, "Do I have this young man's attention?" Most of the teachers vigorously nodded their head. The time to finish the workshop was upon me so I had to tell the teachers how to finish up with this young man. He would only undertake this task of being the best in his classroom if he <u>knew that he could do it</u>. So he was going to have to learn how to listen, to read and comprehend, to take tests, to do homework, and to memorize. But, if the teachers and the young man's mother would use his criteria as the reason to learn these things, the young man would understand and be turned on to learning them.

Another example had to do with a seventh grade student. This student had been a very good student in the elementary grades but when she got into junior high her grades starting slipping to Bs and Cs. Her mother was a school teacher and became alarmed over this change in her daughter and brought her in to see me. The student used to be interested in making good grades and now was not. She also used to be diligent in doing her homework. Now she didn't do her homework on a regular basis and when she did do it, it was poorly done. Her test scores also reflected the lack of effort she was making in her homework.

One thing to remember about students as they develop in their natural growing up process; the different development stages they go through will cause them to focus on different criteria. First, elementary grade students are far more interested in satisfying or pleasing parents then junior high students. Junior high students are almost totally focused on their peers and how they measure up to them and to the number of friends they have or don't have. Second, as students shift from school to school or level to level, they tend to re-evaluate their status unconsciously and to adopt new behaviors which will accommodate their new criteria.

One thing to remember about students as they develop in their natural growing up process; the different development stages they go through will cause them to focus on different criteria.

...as students shift from school to school or level to level, they tend to re-evaluate their status unconsciously and to adopt new behaviors which will accommodate their new criteria.

As I talked to the young lady, it became obvious that she had made the shift to the typical junior high thinking and that her focus was all on her friends. It also became obvious that she had arrived at the belief that good students do not have lots of <u>friends</u>. Since having lots of friends was of paramount importance to her, she was letting her grades slip in order not to be labeled a <u>good student</u>!

Upon further enquiry, I found out how she had arrived at that belief. One day as she and her friends were strolling through the school on their lunch hour, they had noted another young lady sitting off by herself engrossed in a book. The young lady was well known as a straight A student but also as a loner -- somebody who had very few friends, who was withdrawn, and who always was reading a book. One of the girls made a sarcastic remark about the girl which implied that the reason the girl didn't have any friends was that she studied too much. The message jolted my client since having friends was so important to her and she unconsciously resolved to not let that happen to her. Thus, the slipping grades and attitude.

My task was to convince her that having good grades would not keep her from having lots of good friends. I asked her for counter examples. That is, I asked her if she knew of <u>any</u> highly popular girls in her school who were also good students. After several moments of thought she could recall a few. I then asked her if she could tell me the difference between the popular good students and the girl who was not popular. After a few more minutes of thought, she replied that the popular girls were more friendly and outgoing whereas the non-popular girl was very withdrawn.

As we talked about the differences, I continued to emphasize this point that the difference was in the social skills and had nothing to do with being smart or making good grades. I then asked her if she knew how to make good grades. She replied that she did. I then asked her if she knew how to be friendly and outgoing and to make new friends and keep them. She replied that she also knew how to do that. I then suggested to her that she had the best of both worlds and really did not have to make a choice between being good student and having lots of friends, she could have <u>both</u> and that there wasn't any need to limit herself. She agreed. (Author's note--I just ran into the parents of this young lady and they volunteered that she is now a graduate student and doing exceedingly well. She is majoring in Geology!)

One important thing to realize in this last example, as a tactic, is that you don't deny or fight or judge the criteria students are operating out of. If you do, you will simply set up a dogfight that will escalate every time you bring the subject up. What you are trying to do is find out what important criterion they are operating out of and to accept it, even appreciate it, and then show them how school or learning is going to get it for them.

> ...you don't deny or fight or judge the criteria student are operating out of. If you do, you will simply set up a dogfight that will escalate every time you bring the subject up.

If you accept and appreciate their highly valued criteria, they don't need to fight you because you're their ally and they will listen to you. If you judge their highly valued criteria, or tell them they are wrong, you will become an adversary they will have to fight or ignore. If you think they need another more useful criteria to operate out of, you can help them adopt that new criteria if you have rapport with them. If you judge or criticize their criteria, you will lose rapport. If you accept and appreciate their current criteria, you will gain rapport and their acceptance of you as somebody to listen to.

An eighth grade student was brought in on another day. His mother complained that he was not doing as well in school as he should. She stated that when he wanted to do something, he would perform brilliantly, perfectly in fact, but that most of the time he would just get by and do only what he had to do.

...when he wanted to do something, he would perform brilliantly, perfectly in fact, but that most of the time he would just get by and do only what he had to do.

I turned to the student and asked him to give me an example of something he had performed well on. He thought for a moment and replied, "Well I did this report a couple of weeks ago that the teacher really liked." I then asked, "What was it about this particular report that caused you to decide to put out the extra effort?" He stated that it interested him because it would be something he could see a use for. As I talked more to the young man, it became obvious that his criteria for learning something was if he could see any possible use for it. If the usefulness of the task was not apparent to him, he simply turned off his thinking.

I then asked him how, on that particular project, he arrived at the usefulness of the information. He replied, "When the teacher was describing the assignment she told us all the different places we would be able to use it." I asked him to think about other assignments he did not get turned on to and to describe how the teacher had explained the assignment. He replied, "On those assignments, the teacher just told us what she wanted done and when it was due."

Now useful learning is a criteria a lot of people have. But it is not a useful criteria for school children. His problem was compounded by the fact that he relied upon the teacher to provide him the information on how it was going to be useful, rather than his being responsible for finding it. What I wanted the student to do was take responsibility for finding the usefulness of the material the teacher presents. I explained to him what he had been doing and then asked him the following question, "You can either continue to wait for the teacher to accidentally show you the usefulness of a particular lesson, or you can let me teach you how to find the usefulness of lessons. In your opinion, which choice would be more USEFUL to you?" It didn't take him long to decide and I proceeded to teach him some techniques for taking over that responsibility.

> "You can either continue to wait for the teacher to accidentally show you the usefulness of a particular lesson, or you can let me teach you how to find the usefulness of lessons. In your opinion, which choice would be more USEFUL to you?"

I hope it is obvious that the choice I was offering him was designed to appeal to his criteria. I didn't tell him he had to do anything. I just offered him an alternative to what he had been doing and asked him to choose based on his own criteria.

Questions and Answers

Why does this work so easy? -- It seems so simple.

As stated at the beginning, we humans are constantly searching for ways to get what is important to us. We are in a perpetual hunt. We are frustrated when we are not getting our criteria met or when they are violated and we are elated when we are getting criteria met. When a student is forced to participate in school, and school or some aspect of school has not been connected to his criteria, he is in a negative experience. When somebody comes along and shows them a way to not only relieve this negative experience but to turn it into a positive experience, the emotional shift is tremendous! There is no need for them to fight us -- we're helping them. This reason it is so simple is because it is so <u>precise.</u>

Is This Manipulation?

Manipulation occurs when you are trying to force or coerce somebody to do something that he doesn't want to do. Here you're showing him how to get something that he WILL WANT *as soon as you make the connection with*

Manipulation occurs when you are trying to force or coerce somebody to do something that he doesn't want to do.

his highly valued criteria! Furthermore, you can be up front with it. Most people will not try to hide their criteria from you. After all, they think everybody should have these same criteria. They would argue with you that their criteria IS the most important criteria. They may be a little skeptical that you can make the connection. After all, they have never been able to do it-- why should you?

How Do You Figure Out How To Make The Connections?

As stated previously, find an isomorphic activity that the student is already turned on to and find the criteria and/or the way the student thinks about them that is different. This will reveal the information you need to know. How to deliver it to the student is a different matter. Sometimes you can directly ask the student or even challenge him to make the connection. You can do this by comparing the two isomorphic activities overtly and challenging him to make the connection.

In the work I did with the student/golfer (described above), as I was talking about how he practiced golf by himself by trying to hit each shot better and better and overlapped this into doing his Algebra homework, he was moving ahead of me and he started making the connection by surmising that he could try to do his Algebra problems faster and better each time. Again, the student is just as interested in finding the connection as you are. You don't have to hide what you are doing if you have rapport with him.

Another way to help them make the connection, in a more indirect way, is to tell them metaphors. Tell them about other people or students who have the same criteria that they do and tell them how those other students behaved or thought about school. Tell them how those thoughts and behaviors helped them get their criteria satisfied. You might even be the person you describe. Tell what you were like in school and how you turned it around -- IT MUST FIT THEIR CRITERIA, HOWEVER. The more the person you are describing is somebody they admire, the better it is. If you describe a nerd, for example, and they don't like nerds, they will refuse to make the connection.

Will One Statement Do It?

Sometimes, but not always. One statement may start them down the path but there may be pitfalls on the way to being completely turned on. A lot of times, the students may not know how to do some of the possibilities you've opened up and they may not know where to find out. So a lot of your task is to find as many of these "pitfalls" as possible and help students fill them. The more pitfalls you help them deal with, the more they will see the total possibility and be turned on. I think of it as building intensity. The satisfaction of highly valued criteria builds excitement and intensity. Every potential problem or pitfall drains excitement and intensity, therefore, every connection to criteria that is made and every pitfall solved builds excitement and intensity. If I let a student go off on his own, he may get there, but at a much later date. If I can offer help and resources, I can speed up the journey. If I have used an isomorphic experience in his life

> I think of it as building intensity. The satisfaction of highly valued criteria builds excitement and intensity. Every potential problem or pitfall drains excitement and intensity, therefore, every connection to criteria that is made and every pitfall solved builds excitement and intensity.

to make some of the connections and if that isomorphism is complete, the answers for the student already exists in the isomorphism. Sometimes you can point that out to a student.

Do Students Ever Object To The Connections You Are Trying To Make?

They will if the connection hasn't been made yet. Prior to the final moment when what you're trying to connect gets connected, they will sometimes resist or want to be argumentive. And it makes sense -- how can they get excited about something that hasn't connected yet? A lot of this depends on your rapport skills. If you have a lot of rapport with them, they will tend to be less argumentive and resistant. Also, you have to make sure the connection you are striving for fits their criteria and way of thinking about things and NOT YOURS. <u>Be sure you keep your criteria out of it.</u> That is why using one of their isomorphic experiences is so valuable. It gives you a blueprint for how they do it in other like type situations.

They will also object if the new situation is too overwhelming and/or they perceive too many problems. It is important, in this situation, to be patient and walk them through the solutions until the enormity of the task and the unfamiliarity of the new situation is dealt with. There are also students who like to figure things out for themselves. They will resist you doing it for them. Being patient, using metaphors or stories about yourself and other students you know about will work with these types of students. You have to be sure they don't realize you are trying to give them answers, though.

What Are Ways To Find The Pitfalls?

Be creative with your own mind and imagine yourself in the student's shoes with the questions in your mind of "What is this like? What do I need to know and be able to do to accomplish this? What potential problems am I going to have? How is my life going to be different and how am I going to deal with it? What am I having to give up to accomplish this?" As you ask yourself and the student these questions, you and he can brainstorm answers. Remember, you can use his own isomorphism to find the answers and to reassure the student that he has passed this way before.

Another way to elicit potential pitfalls is by what we call "future-pacing." In effect, you have the student imagine that he is doing the new behaviors in the near future. You have him imagine what it would be like. "Are you comfortable? Do you know what to do? Do you like the results? Are there any additional pitfalls you encountered which need attention now?" As you walk him through several instances in his future, you are accomplishing several very worthwhile things. One, you are checking for potential problems. But more importantly, you are familiarizing him with how it is going to be. It will now no longer be so strange and scary for him because he has been there and practiced the new behaviors.

Keeping Them Turned On

Is it possible that once we have turned them on to school and learning that they will lose that desire? Yes!! Remember the story of the seventh grade girl who was turned off of school because she thought good students didn't have friends. The inadvertent comment by one of her friends had an instant impact on her (because it appealed to her higher criteria). There are several times and situations in a student's life that bear watching as potential trouble spots. You, as a parent or teacher, can be alert to these situations and intervene if you think it is necessary.

One of the most frustrating situations for many parents and teachers is the fleeting motivation and commitment to doing well in school some students exhibit. One week or year or semester they are highly motivated and committed and do exceedingly well in school. But the next moment they seem to completely "blow off" school as "not important". Parents and teachers figuratively tear out their hair trying to figure out these fickle and fleeting moments of motivation and achievement.

Personal commitment to doing well in school occurs when:

- the student realizes how doing well in school serves his own personal standards of importance (his own "highly valued criteria").

- the student knows **HOW** to successfully do the classroom tasks which are required of him.

- personal emotional or mental problems at school, home, in the family, or in relationships are not present which "override" the importance of doing well in school.

When a student does well in school, **ALL** of the above factors will be present. Divorce, deaths, and other personal tragedies are obviously traumatic to children and adults and can and will affect commitment. There are, however, other more subtle factors at play in the fickle commitment of students, as follows:

1. Chance comments: As in the case of the seventh grade student mentioned previously; chance comments of friends, relatives, or other teachers can always have the potential to hook a highly valued criteria. This is particularly true as they move from one developmental stage to another or is in some other transition period in which their criteria may be changing.

One of the ways to remedy this is for you to be alert for these comments and to appeal to an even higher criteria. As mentioned before, asking "What is important about (criteria) to you?" will move up in the hierarchy of criteria. You can keep repeating this question until the student can't find anything more important. The higher valued criteria will cover more contexts then the lower criteria. Lower valued criteria tend to be specialized to particular situations or contexts. The student has less of a tendency to give up on the higher valued criteria.

Another way to get at higher valued criteria of a student is to ask yourself the question, "What kind of person would have these kinds of criteria?" You can check out your guess by feeding it back to the student in the form of the following comments: "You seem like the kind of person who would_____! Or, it seems to me that _____ would be important to you! Or, You are the kind of person who believes _____ is important!" If you have hit criteria that are important to him, you will be able to tell it from his response. Now you can make the connection of school or learning to this higher criteria.

2. Their Interest Shifts: Surprise! If as they mature their criteria shift, so will their interests. So if you have turned them on to school based on a previous criteria and interest, when they shift, you need to make new connections based upon their new criteria and interests.

3. Their Self-image Changes: This is not only possible through developmental stages, but through traumatic experiences they may have in their personal life. Their parents may get a divorce or somebody close to them may die or get real sick -- or their self-image may slowly evolve into something else. People commit to things or situations which are consistent with their self-image. So, if at one time the student committed himself to school based on his old image and then the image changed, the commitment is lost.

> So, if at one time the student committed himself to school based on his old image and then the image changed, the commitment is lost.

4. Doing The Nitty, Gritty: A lot of us can get turned on to lofty goals. We like the big picture and can get excited about it. But when it comes time to do what it takes to do it, some of us are less then excited. Students in school are the same way. There are a lot of very specific and sometimes boring tasks that have to be done to be successful in school. These little tasks are not in and of themselves very motivating, so students procrastinate on them and after awhile develop a bad attitude about the tasks. Sometimes these little tasks can contaminate their whole attitude about school in general. Examples of these types of tasks are; doing class work on a daily basis, listening in class, doing repetitive homework, taking tests, following instructions, and sitting still. The way to motivate a student to do these types of tasks is to make sure he sees the contribution the tasks will make to getting the highly valued criteria met. Once that connection has been made, the tasks have meaning and the student doesn't mind them as much.

5. Knowing How To Do The Tasks: Its one thing to know what to do to get your criteria met. Its another thing to know HOW to do it. So many times in school we assume students know how to do the little things necessary to succeed. In my experience, many students do not know how and since they don't want to look like fools, they don't ask questions. For example, how do you find repetitive homework interesting? How do you listen to teachers and make it interesting? How do you find usefulness in all the subject matter that is being taught? How do you motivate yourself? How do you "try harder"? How do you memorize large amounts of data?

6. Wanting To Do The Tasks: Knowing what to do and how to do it are still not all the considerations that are important. Sometimes we know what to do and how to do it but <u>we don't want to do it</u>! This is closely akin to knowing how; it's just knowing how to enjoy doing something. A lot of people want to be healthy and have a firm

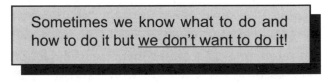

Sometimes we know what to do and how to do it but <u>we don't want to do it</u>!

body through exercise. They even know what exercise to do <u>and</u> how to do it; they just don't like it! So, they don't!

Students are the same way in school. There are some tasks we ask them to do that are boring and even distasteful. To teach students how to enjoy these tasks is doing them a real favor. One primary source of how to do this is in the isomorphic experiences you find in the student. Examples we have previously covered include the secretary who didn't like exercise and the golfer who didn't like repetitive homework.

7. Setting Goals Too Low: Another way to lose commitment is to accomplish what you have set out to accomplish. You can't keep up the intensity if you accomplish the goal. Furthermore, when the intensity goes away, it is hard to resurrect. Think of people who commit to diets. If they say "I'm going to lose X number of pounds!" and then do it, they really feel good. But what do they do next? Typically, they start to gain it back and it is hard to recharge the commitment. One has to set a long-term goal to commit to. Such as "I'm going to lose X pounds and <u>keep</u> it off." If a parent, for example, says to a student, I will pay you $X for every A you bring home, the student says to himself, "If I make As, I can get that bike I want!" When he gets enough money for the bike, guess what happens to his motivation?

Another example of short-term motivation is when a student is turned on to doing well because he wants to please a particular teacher. The student seems to be really inspired to do well as long as he has that particular teacher. The danger in this is when the student or the teacher moves on it is really difficult to get motivated again. Furthermore, now the student and his parents know he can do it, and the pressure builds for him to do it again. But the quality of the experience is different now for the student. It's tough for him to rebuild the momentum and regain the intensity he had before. As the pressure builds, guilt trips and bad feelings get worse and the student starts to doubt his abilities to do well in school.

One of the ways to avoid this is to appeal school and/or learning to either higher valued criteria or to the students' self-image. Most good students do well in school because doing well in school is THEM. It would be inconsistent with their self-image NOT to do well. In fact, they think of school as their arena in which they get to achieve. It's the place where they can accomplish things and feel good about it. This type of thinking makes every test and assignment a challenge or opportunity.

8. **Dependent Upon Other People:** Sometimes students will commit to school or learning as long as somebody else is involved. We've already covered if they are committed to learning because of a specific teacher. But also some

students will build study routines around friends. They may have a group of friends who study together and have a lot of fun. In fact, the routine may be initiated by a specific person in the group. If the group is lost or disrupted in some way, the motivation to study may mysteriously disappear. I once worked with a college student who had flunked out of college for this very reason. In high school he had a group of friends who were very good students and who studied together. His friends went to other colleges and he went to a college by himself. For some reason he couldn't get himself to study because he had never had to study as an individual. Another way to become dependent on another person is by being motivated to make higher grades than he makes; to compete with him. This may work well until the other student is no longer around. When the competitive spirit goes, the commitment to school may also go.

9. Learning Routines Disrupted: When some students commit to any long-term goal, one of the first things that happens is they start to figure out HOW they are going to accomplish the task. They set up routines which, if they work, become habits. After a while, these study routines become THE WAY to get studying done. When the routines get disrupted, the reaction of some students is that they <u>can't</u> study. They can become very distraught and, if pressure is applied, an argument can ensue. Examples of these types of routines are; studying in a particular place or at a particular time, playing music while studying, studying with somebody else, or studying in a particular way (like having a set time to study before a test). The remedy is to realize that a study routine has been disrupted and to re-think and to re-decide a new routine.

10. Transition Times: Some of the most dangerous times to long term commitment are in the natural transition times which occur in all our lives.

Some of the most dangerous times to long term commitment are in the natural transition times which occur in all our lives.

For students some of these naturally occurring times are: when moving from one school to another; when moving from one grade to another (particularly if there are a lot of unknowns); when moving from one major level to another, e.g., beginning school, from elementary school to junior high, from junior high to high school, and from high school to college, and from college to citizen. It seems that in all these transition times, particularly when the upcoming is VERY unknown, we do a lot of re-thinking about what to expect and how we are going to behave. Since this re-thinking is about getting what is important to us (our criteria) at the time, if school and learning has been defined in terms of lower criteria and the re-thinking is in terms of higher criteria, then commitment to school and doing well in school may go down the drain.

The danger signs which signal parents and teachers that a student is going through this kind of experience are major shifts in attitude, behavior problems and/or apathy. Parents can also be alert at the major transition times in their child's life and be ready to offer different ways to think and feel about doing well in school which are more conducive to the new stage.

Parents can also be alert at the major transition times in their child's life and be ready to offer different ways to think and feel about doing well in school which are more conducive to the new stage.

LEARNING STYLES

Learning Styles are not new to the educational system. They have been taught to teachers and talked about for many years. Most of the learning style theory, however, has been limited to whether a student was visual, or auditory, or kinesthetic. In this section, I want to greatly expand the concept and range of learning styles.

When we talk about learning styles, we are referring to the unique ways in which a particular person learns -- his preferred style. As noted earlier, the modality through which the student received and processed information (i. e., visual, auditory, and kinesthetic) has been the primary focus.

One of the key skills of an excellent communicator is his ability to be flexible in his communication style and to adjust to the communication styles of different people -- particularly when the other person is having difficulty adjusting to the communicator. They do this by picking up on subtle verbal and non-verbal cues from the other person which lets them know how the person needs the communication delivered. One way to think about how to use these learning style skills is in terms of the question, "To what is the other person paying attention?" You then deliver your communication in a way that they pay attention to your communication. Good teachers can do the same thing with the learning process. They recognize that the student is focused on some other facet of the lesson to be learned (and, in fact, may be stuck in that focus) and they adjust their teaching to match where the student is focused or they assist the student in re-focusing.

> The following sections on learning styles give you some guidelines on what to look for and on how to make your adjustment.

Visual or Auditory or Kinesthetic

When students are paying attention to what they can see -- they are being visual. When they are paying attention to feelings or their body, they are being kinesthetic. When they are paying attention to sounds, they are being auditory.

When we think and learn, we process our experiences and information in one or more of our senses. We can visually process by making pictures in our head. We can auditorially process by talking to ourselves and internally repeating conversations or other sounds. We can kinesthetically process by accessing and/ or remembering emotions or body sensations.

For the students who are visually processing, it will help communication if you will assist them in painting a picture in their mind. It will also help if you will use sensory based words or predicates that are visual in nature. A few of the many visual predicates are; look, see, picture, clear, vision, light, shine, reveal, image, view, appear, show, watch, and focus. One of the ways you will know they are visually processing is by listening to the visual predicates they are using. You simply match their visual predicates in your response.

Visual students learn best when they can "see" what is to be learned. They respond well to movies, video tapes, and demonstrations. It is helpful if visual students realize that they can make up the pictures when the lesson is not automatically given to them in a visual format.

When students are auditorially processing, you will hear them use some of the auditory predicates such as; hear, say, talk, discuss, praise, call, noise, argue, quiet, speak, listen, tone, and sound. These are just a few of the many auditory predicates that are available. To strengthen rapport and to help them understand or learn, you simply match their auditory predicates in your response to them.

Auditory students learn best when they can talk about the subject matter. Therefore, discussions and question/answer types of classes appeal to them. Auditory students like to study with other students so they can talk about the subject matter and ask questions of each other.

Kinesthetic processors use predicates, such as; feel, tough, solid, unbalanced, warm, rough, tension, connect, smooth, support, firm, twist, touch, and soft -- to name just a few. Again, you simply match the types of predicates they use to gain rapport and to help them learn with their unique learning style. Kinesthetic students like to DO things. They like to move their bodies. They are the classic "hands on" learner. They, therefore, like to learn anything that is active or physical.

Another way to determine how the other person is processing information and experience is to watch their eye accessing cues. When a person looks, with unfocused eyes, to one of the six locations as indicated in the figure on the next page, they will be accessing visually, auditorially, or kinesthetically as indicated.

When they need help with the learning process or look confused, and if you see them look up to their left or right, you know you need to help them form internal images of the material. When they look down to their left or straight to their left or right, you can assist them auditorially by having them repeat back to you the material or by explaining it in a different manner. If they look down to the right, you know they need to have a "feel" for the material or they are ready to "do it" or get their body involved.

This pattern of eye accessing is true for a large percentage of the population. Left handed individuals will sometimes reverse the pattern from left to right. People with mixed dominance may have their own unique eye accessing pattern. You can ask them specially designed questions to determine their unique pattern.

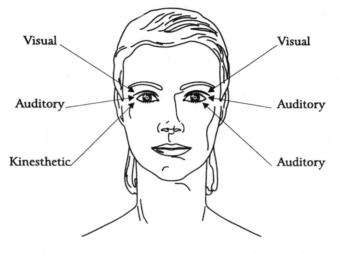

Visual   Visual

Auditory   Auditory

Kinesthetic   Auditory

Student's Right   Student's Left

Toward Pleasure or Away From Pain

Another distinction to notice is whether a person is an "away from pain" person or a "toward pleasure" person. This distinction has a lot to do with motivation or their desire to do a project or to learn something. The "away from pain" person responds to deadlines -- sometimes waiting until the last minute to do things. The "toward pleasure" person is a goal setter who sets the goal and its rewards as something to be drawn toward.

A person who is "away from pain" responds more strongly to negative consequences or the threat of punishment. He will ask, "What will happen to me if I do or don't do this?" If the perceived threat is bad enough, he will become motivated. An "away from pain" person will not pay any attention to the awards or rewards of doing something. Many parents and teachers will try to motivate students to study for a test by talking to them about how good they will feel if they do well, or what others will think about them, or may even offer money for good grades. To an "away from pain" student, these inducements are not motivating at all.

The "toward pleasure" student, however, responds well to those kinds of inducements. The "toward pleasure" person is asking the question "what's in it for me?" They do not respond well to threats of punishment or of dire consequences. Many parents will attempt to motivate students by telling them how terrible it will be to flunk a test, how everybody will think badly about them if they flunk, or how badly they will feel.

> The "toward pleasure" person is asking the question, "What's in it for me?"

The "toward pleasure" student shrugs these comments off and says "who cares!" The "away from pain" student, however, will respond to these types of comments.

Imagine a scenario where a student, who has a upcoming test, is watching a favorite TV program. His parents are trying to get her to study for the test. She thinks studying is boring and really doesn't study too well anyway. The parents continue to pressure her into studying. The "away from pain" student will think about the pain of studying and compare it to the pain of hearing the parents nag him. The student will move <u>away</u> from whichever is the greatest pain. If the parents threaten her enough she may eventually start studying. She also will study if somebody shows her how to lessen the boredom and pain of studying. The parents, therefore, have three choices. They can increase the pain of watching TV, lessen the pain of studying, or do both.

The "toward pleasure" student, in the same scenario, will think about the pleasure of watching his favorite TV program and compare it with the pleasure of studying for the test and move ***toward*** whichever is greatest. The parents' three choices in this case are to lessen the pleasure of watching TV (maybe turn it off), increase the pleasure of studying for the test (maybe by teaching the student a better way to study), or do both.

Fear, failure, threats and negative consequences will dominate the language of the "away from pain" person. Pleasure, rewards, benefits, and positive consequences will dominate the language of the "toward pleasure" person.

These distinctions are detected in language patterns when a person is talking about the motivation of doing things. Fear, failure, threats, and negative consequences will dominate the language of the "away from pain" person. Pleasure, rewards, benefits, and positive consequences will dominate the language of the "toward pleasure" person.

Externally or Internally Oriented

Another distinction to notice and to adjust to in your communication with others is whether they are an externally oriented or an internally oriented person. That is, what information do they give the most credibility to -- information which comes from others -- from outside themselves or information they create on their own. This is not about being an introvert or extrovert. This is about the source of information and how they respond to it.

Internally oriented people resist when somebody offers them an idea, even if it is a good idea. They become motivated if the idea is theirs. They want to own the idea. If offered an idea, you will hear them say, "Let me think about it; or mull it over; or chew on it for awhile; or sleep on it." And they will go inside their head

> Internally oriented people resist when somebody offers them an idea, even if it is a good idea.

and not talk to anybody about it for hours, days, or even weeks. Then they will typically come to you with "their own better version." If you push them for a response before they are ready, they will usually become resistant.

Externally oriented people, on the other hand, like suggestions or to be told what to do and how to do it. They place more credence on information that comes from outside themselves than what they can figure out for themselves. They also give ownership to whoever gives them the information. These are people who want guidance from the outside. They will willingly ask for your advice. In fact, they will not be motivated until they get advice from others.

Internally oriented people like to figure things out so they are good working by themselves where they have to make the decisions. They are not very good at taking orders or at "going by the book". Externally oriented people love the policy manuals or regulations which tell them exactly what to do. They are not good at working by themselves "in the field or individual study project" where they have to figure things out themselves.

Since our schools and the typical instructional method is so externally oriented, many internal students have a rough time following instructions and doing things by the book. Sometimes the natural resistance this elicits gets in their way of performing satisfactorily. Later on, when they become business men or women who work in corporations or other type bureaucracies which have

Since our schools and the typical instructional method is so externally oriented, many internal students have a rough time following instructions and doing things by the book.

extensive policy manuals or operate from the top down, they will also struggle with constantly being told what to do. They will sometimes suffer burnout or ulcers or other physical maladies because of the stress that the internally oriented go through in this environment.

So, how do we communicate with these two types of individuals? The externally oriented are easy -- you just tell or show them what you want them to do. The major problem most people have with externally oriented persons is they get tired of having to do their thinking for them. We wish they would leave us alone. The internally oriented person is

The major problem most people have with externally oriented persons is they get tired of having to do their thinking for them.

much more difficult. They *will* leave us alone -- often for great periods of time. We don't know what they are thinking or where they are in the process of figuring something out.

If we want to give the internally oriented an idea, we have to "plant a seed" of the idea and then leave them alone and let them figure out what to do. We also have to allow them to think it is their idea when they come back to us with "this great idea". If you respond to their idea with, "I told you that the other day", they will instantly rebel.

The potential conflicts between these two types of individuals are numerous and sometimes very emotional. The internally oriented wish the externally would think for themselves and leave them alone. The externally oriented wish the internally oriented would talk to them more and share what they want and what they are thinking.

The internally oriented wish the externally would think for themselves and leave them alone. The externally oriented wish the internally oriented would talk to them more and share what they want and what they are thinking.

General -- Specific

The learning style discussed in this section is not only a great source of irritation between and among certain types of individuals but is a cause of much discontent in school and is one of the reasons some students are labeled "learning disabled."

It has to do with the "chunk size" of information we can process and which we like to process. When we discuss something, we can talk about it in very general terms or we can talk about it in highly specific terms. In fact, there is a continuum in chunk size from the very general to the very specific. We can choose to talk and process information any place on the continuum. The person we are talking to, however, may have a preference as to how general or specific she or he wants the conversation. If we mis-match this preference, it can become very irritating to the other person.

On one end of the continuum is the general person. This type of person likes to see the BIG picture, the trends, the patterns, the causes and effects. He typically dislikes details or ignore them. At the very least, he will not process the specifics until he can see how they relate to the big picture.

At the other end of the continuum is the highly specific person. This person thrives on details and facts and disdains the generalist as having "no substance." This person tends to be much more practical then the generalist. He likes to deal with "hard data" and can be annoyed when a generalist does not get down to the "bottom line."

Both of these types are needed and serve a great purpose solving problems and in getting things done. They complement each other very well and, in fact, they need each other. A problem occurs if they cannot momentarily adjust their chunk size to communicate with the other person. Some become rigid in thinking that their way of learning and communicating is the "right and only way" to do it. They then lose their sense of acceptance and appreciation for how the other person complements them. Major communication problems can then occur.

In schools and in the learning process, this pattern can cause many types of problems. Some subjects tend to be more detail oriented. Other subjects tend to be more general -- same for the teachers. If a detail student is in a class where the subject matter is general or the teacher is a generalist, learning or behavior or morale problems can occur if the student does not know how to adjust. The reverse is obviously just as true.

If a detail student is in a class where the subject matter is general or the teacher is a generalist, learning or behavior or morale problems can occur if the student does not know how to adjust. The reverse is obviously just as true.

How many times have parents heard their children complain about the fact that a teacher makes them write down all the steps to a math problem -- a generalist's complaint. Or that a student gets in trouble when she asks "Why are we studying this?" -- a generalist's question. Or, "Where will I use this?" -- a specific's question. Or, "Can you give me an example of that?" -- another specific's question.

In reality, students need to be able to "chunk up" to the general or "chunk down" to specifics in order to be a well rounded student. Learning successfully in school and comprehension require this easily learned academic skill. Also, teachers and parents need to be able to adjust the chunk size of their presentations and communication to aid the student in this endeavor.

Matchers or Mis-matchers

We learn by looking for similarities or differences. When we are looking for similarities we notice patterns -- how things match up. This allows us to make generalizations, notice trends and patterns, see cause/effects, etc. When we look for differences, we are looking for exceptions, for loop holes, for mismatches. This allows us to notice the distinctions that really make a difference.

The people who learns by noticing similarities (sometimes called a matcher) will ask questions like "How is this like _____?" or "Is this the same as ____?" The individuals of this type tend to go along with what you are saying. As long as they can match what you're saying with something that makes sense or something they already know about, they are satisfied. These are pretty easy going students to have in class. They don't ask a lot of hard questions.

The person who looks for differences, however, typically has a different effect on us. This person will look for what is missing. They will look for loopholes -- for what can go wrong. These people are sometimes labeled the "yes, but ..." people. We have all attempted to communicate with people of this type. Other labels for this type of person are "mis-matcher", "exception finder" and "counter example finder."

The mis-matchers are thought to "nitpick" things to death -- particularly if they are highly specific and detailed individuals.

The matchers will be convinced of something or know they know something when they can match it with something else they already know. The mis-matchers are convinced or know they know it when **ALL** of the exceptions are found and dealt with. The matchers are fairly easy, therefore, to convince. The mis-matchers are thought to "nitpick" things to death -- particularly if they are highly specific and detailed individuals.

If you ask matchers a simple question, such as, "Do you like this class?", they will quickly find evidence to match the question and immediately respond "Of course I like it!" If you ask mis-matchers the same question, they will hesitate while they check out **ALL** of the exceptions, such as, "I didn't like this part of it this morning -- can I accept that?" or "Is the argument from last week resolved yet?" Meanwhile, the person who asked the mis-matcher the question is left wondering what the delay in the answer is all about.

The matchers are easier to convince but the next person they talk to may convince them of something else -- they are therefore more fickle and less reliable. The mis-matchers will take longer to convince but usually once they have made up their mind, they are very difficult to change. If you are trying to convince a mis-matcher of something, it is best to elicit as many exceptions as you can in order to be available to help him answer his questions. If he leaves your presence and an exception occurs to him and he can't answer it, he may start to waver.

Classrooms need both kinds of learners. They each provide a needed perspective and serve a useful purpose in the learning process. If you have a classroom full of matchers, nobody looks out for the unusual or loopholes or the things that could go wrong. That's usually the role of the mis-matcher. If you have a classroom full of mis-matchers, the learning process is going to be longer and less structured because EVERYBODY

> If you have a classroom full of mis-matchers, the learning process is going to be longer and less structured because EVERYBODY will be going off track, looking for exceptions and the lesson plan can get lost in the process.

will be going off track, looking for exceptions and the lesson plan can get lost in the process.

Obviously, students who are mis-matchers have a rough time in the typical classroom because they demand a lot of time from the teacher. They are sometimes thought to be trouble makers because they ask so many questions. This is, however, their way of totally learning and comprehending a concept.

> **Obviously, students who are mis-matchers have a rough time in the typical classroom because they demand a lot of time from the teacher. They are sometimes thought to be trouble makers because they ask so many questions.**

Convincer Styles

This section is about how a student knows when he knows something -- when he is convinced that he knows it. It cuts across some of the other learning styles outlined here and is pretty much an individual preference.

Matcher -- The matcher is convinced of something when it can be compared to something he already knows is true -- when he can find the similarities.

Mis-matcher -- The mis-matcher is convinced when ALL exceptions have answers -- when he can diligently search through his mind and find NO loopholes.

Visual -- The visual person has to have visual evidence of the concept or item to be learned. It may be real evidence he can see or it can be a picture in his mind.

Auditory -- The auditory person will be convinced when he hears somebody else confirm the learning or say that he is convinced it is true. He will also be convinced if he can fluidly talk about it or teach it.

Kinesthetic -- The kinesthetic person is convinced when he can FEEL the evidence. He may have to physically do something with the learning creating a hands-on project. He also can be convinced if he can have an emotional attachment to the learning.

Number of Examples -- Some students require a specified number of examples before they are convinced something is true. It can range from 1 to 50 or over. Of course the visuals have to see the examples, the auditory students have to hear them, etc.

Over Time -- Some students have to have a set amount of time to pass before they are convinced something is true. This is the "time will tell" cliché that we hear from some students. Each of these students will have his own amount of time he needs and if he doesn't have the luxury of that amount of time he will remain unconvinced.

Generalists -- Students who tend to be general thinkers are not usually convinced until they can "see the big picture" and how the specifics fit into it. Details by themselves are meaningless to the generalists. They need to have a purpose for learning the details.

Detailers -- Students who focus on details get lost when the lesson is "blue sky" or philosophical. Detail students become convinced when "practical and hard core data" is presented.

Variety or Routine

This learning style has to do with how exciting or boring some things are -- also, how well we do certain tasks. In school, there are repetitive tasks to do which HAVE to be done in order to be successful. Some students, however, don't like repetitive tasks -- the kind of task in which it is known what to do and is done the same way every time. That translates as boring to the variety student. The student who likes routines, however, is in his element because he knows what to do and there are no surprises. The predictability of the routine gives him a secure feeling.

The variety students will deliberately change the routines or disobey the instructions in order to inject some variety into a situation. They love the tasks in which they can change things around and do them differently every time. They love risks and will sometimes do things against the rules or instructions simply because to not do so would be boring.

> They love risks and will sometimes do things against the rules or instructions simply because to not do so would be boring.

Variety students love classrooms and teachers in which the lessons are always different and where the class routine is varied and unpredictable. When "you never know what's going to happen!" In a classroom where the teacher has set routines and strict rules of behavior, however, they get restless and tend to get into trouble. They also get into trouble when the teacher has a set way to do something and wants the students to follow the procedure to the letter of the law.

The routine student, on the other hand, is always asking the teacher exactly how she wants it done. Or, he will determine in his own mind a best way to do something and then do it that way every time. When an exception to their procedure occurs, he becomes upset and doesn't know what to do until a new routine is established.

Less Occurring Learning Styles

The following learning styles tend to occur on special occasions and do not dominate the students ability to learn like the ones previously covered:

Time Orientation -- Students will orient themselves in time according to past, present, or future. Where they are oriented will tend to allow them to favor certain subjects which cater to their orientation. For example, past oriented students will like history while future oriented will not. Future oriented may really like science or computers or high tech learning while past oriented students will not. Past oriented students like tradition and like to keep doing things the way they have always been done. Future oriented students abhor tradition and want to learn the information of the future. Present oriented students tend not to be turned on unless the subject matter is usable or relevant "right now."

Self or Other -- Does the student tend to focus on others or is the focus on what is happening to him? More importantly, does he exclude others and focus on himself or does he exclude himself and totally focus on others in his life? Self-focused students tend to be truer to their own feelings and thoughts and are relatively insensitive as to how others might feel or think. While, in contrast, other-focused students are exceptionally sensitive and considerate of others while denying their own feelings, thoughts and needs.

Content Sorts -- When the student is paying attention to the world around him, what content does he search for? What content does he pay attention to? For example, if you were describing your day to him, he would ask questions such as the following:
> **persons** -- "*Who* were you with?"
> **places** -- "*Where* did you go?"
> **activity** -- "*What* did you do?"

> **reason** -- "*Why* did you do that?"
> **process** -- "*How* did you do that?"
> **time** -- "*When* did you do that?"

So, if you are lecturing on history, for example, and are focusing on the people of an era, you will turn some of the students on and not the others. They will tend to be more interested and to ask questions according to their preferred content sort.

Boundaries of Necessity or Possibility or Contingency -- This learning style reflects the <u>structure</u> of the internal model of the subject to be learned that the student has in his mind; particularly the boundaries of that internal world.

The Necessity Person has rigid boundaries in the way he thinks about things. He wants everything to be set in concrete. He wants to be certain. He wants everything to be bound up in a neat package with no loose ends or remaining questions. His language patterns are dominated with words such as; have to, must, got to, and should, or the negative of these; must not and should not, etc. He dislikes uncertainty, unanswered questions, or unfinished projects. His body language, gestures, and tonalities tend to be rigid and closed as well.

The Possibility Person has expanding boundaries. His internal model is flowing and constantly opening up to new possibilities and choices. He abhors rigidity and closed minds. His language patterns are dominated with words such as possibilities, options, choices, abilities, capabilities, and can do, or the negatives of these; cannot, or no options. His body language, gestures, and tonalities tend to be open, flowing and uplifting.

The Contingency Person has no boundaries. His internal model is without shape or form. He will constantly adjust to your model -- like a chameleon. Everything he thinks or does is dependent upon responding to others and reacting. He does not like being pinned down or having to take a stand. His language patterns are dominated with words like; might, could be, try, maybe, and probably. His body language and tonalities are fluid and non-definite or non-formed. His gestures tend to be with uplifted hands, palms up and shrugging shoulders. Also, the body language and gestures will be angular and non-symmetrical.

Thinking or Feeling or Doing

-- Another learning style has to do with our preferring to think about the subject, to become emotionally involved with it, or to have to do something with our body. Some students can get lost in their thoughts about certain subjects and love the subjects that get them to think complicated thoughts -- the more they have to think the better they like it. Others don't like "being in their head" all the time and become turned on when they can be emotionally involved in the subject. It then becomes "important" to them. Some others become more motivated when they can involve their bodies or hands in learning the information or in doing a project -- there has to be action. They don't like to sit and listen to theory, they want to be busy or to do something.

LEARNING DISABILITIES

A Different Presupposition for Understanding Learning Disabilities

Many times when a student is having trouble in school, the parents will take him to various specialists to determine what is wrong. After many examinations and tests, the verdict will come back, "He has a learning disability." Sometimes, the learning disability will have a specific name such as "Dyslexia" or "Attention Deficit Disorder (ADD)", etc. Other times the diagnosis will be "He just seems to learn at a different pace than his peers -- maybe he will grow out of it."

In many cases, the diagnosis is followed by a specific treatment that is not looked upon with much optimism. With ADD, most children are medicated with drugs such as Ritalin to help them focus. Sometimes behavior modification techniques are used to control behavior. Practically all learning disability students are moved to special classes and given special attention usually consisting of a slowed down curriculum and a lower teacher/ student ratio.

Practically all learning disability students are moved to special classes and given special attention usually consisting of a slowed down curriculum and a lower teacher/ student ratio.

Neuro-Linguistic Programming (NLP) offers a wonderful opportunity to make a real difference in a large number of students' lives. NLP offers skills and processes which allow us to uncover the internal processing of these students and discover how they attempt to learn and HOW it is different than other students. We then have the opportunity to teach these students different ways to use their minds so that they will work far better than before.

> ...the missing step seems so minor and yet its absence is so profoundly important. The preciseness of the intervention seems to produce very significant results.

In fact, in my research into learning disabilities, I usually find a relatively simple missing step which most of us have taken for granted and don't even realize it. The step has always been easy to teach once its absence has been found and the results are amazing since the missing step seems so minor and yet its absence is so profoundly important. The preciseness of the intervention seems to produce very significant results.

The new presupposition is that there are missing steps in the internal processing which interfere with the accomplishment of academic tasks. There is usually nothing genetically or logically wrong with the child. There is no dread disease which needs to be treated. It's simply a missing step (or steps) which need to be ferreted out and taught to the child. **The secondary presupposition** is that we can find these missing steps and teach them to the student thereby giving them better strategies for solving the tasks of school and life. Neuro-Linguistic Programming (NLP) offers real hope in dealing with these students in a new way since it offers the very tools needed to uncover the missing steps and in designing and teaching new strategies to these students.

Dyslexia

Its Structure

Sometimes a student with dyslexia symptoms will interchange the letter b and d or the 6 for a 9, for example. The situation usually follows this pattern: a parent or teacher will tell the student to write a b and the student will guess one of the choices and write it down (the student has a 50/50 chance to guess right). What the student with dyslexia symptoms does is say the letter to himself and guess. What the rest of us do is take the sound of the b and make a internal image of it (you can also kinesthetically do this) and then copy the image off on to the paper. The student with dyslexia symptoms does not have an internal image connected to the sound of the letter b -- so the sound does not produce the image.

Students with dyslexia symptoms will also reverse certain words. They will literally read the word from right to left instead of left to right. For example, they will pronounce the word <u>saw</u> as <u>was</u>. This is simply a matter of knowing right from left and in knowing that words CAN ONLY correctly be read from left to right (in the English Language) and in programming their mind to read only from left to right.

Some Techniques for Helping Students With Dyslexia Symptoms

When I teach students with dyslexia symptoms how to know the difference between the letters b and d, for example, I go through the following steps:
1. Show them the letter and tell them to make a picture of it in their mind (e.g. the letter b).
2. **<u>WHILE</u>** they are looking at THEIR INTERNAL IMAGE have them sound out the letter and slightly flex the right side of the body (the side where the loop is).

3. Have them practice this connection 8 to 10 times over several days.

This process connects the visual, auditory, and kinesthetic representations together at the logical level. Later, when you say draw the letter b, the picture and muscle memory are accessed with the sound. You do the same thing for the letter d, except use the left side of the body. The kinesthetic part of the above process is actually redundant and not needed. I use it at first, however, to be sure the student has a positive learning experience. Sometimes they haven't had very many positive learning experiences and need more of them.

When I work with students with dyslexia symptoms who read words backwards (e.g., they read saw as was), I teach them two processes (if they don't already know them): 1) how to tell which hand is the left hand, and 2) a strategy for always reading from left to right.

If they do not know left from right, I teach them this in the following manner:
  a. Have them take an internal picture of their left hand -- noticing particularly where the thumb is located.
  b. WHILE they are looking at the internal image I have them say the word "left" while I am simultaneously touching them on the left forearm or as they flex the left arm.
  c. Have them practice this 8 to 10 times over several days (they will have to remember my touch on their arm).

Have them repeat the process (with appropriate adjustments) for their right hand. I then open a book and say to them "When you read, you always read from left to right" as I touch both forearms in the proper sequence. I then have them say left to right several times while they image the left hand and then the right hand and feel slight muscle tension in first the left forearm then in the right forearm.

The last step is to have them open a book and just before they start to read they repeat the sequence and they read from left to right. They will need to practice this last step -- opening the book, saying/seeing/feeling left to right, and then reading left to right at least 8 to 10 times over several days.

There are many other interventions possible utilizing some creativity and the modeling skills of NLP. These two complaints are the most common I have encountered for Dyslexia. I am sure as more students present themselves to me and to other NLP practitioners that this list of interventions and strategies will increase significantly. I think the possibilities are endless and look forward to hearing from others on their successes.

Attention Deficit Disorder (ADD)

Imagine you are watching a multiple slide show.   You know the kind, where 3 to 5 slide projectors are set up projecting images on a screen. Now imagine that you are asked to report, either verbally or written, on what you are seeing while you are watching it. Frustrating? That's an understatement. And that's exactly how the student with ADD symptoms feels. Now, to make it even more challenging, imagine that the pace of the slide presentation begins to increase, faster and faster. Yet you're still trying to report on what you're seeing. And for the final blow to your sanity, imagine the slides' images start to fly around and flash simultaneously **AND** your emotional well being depends upon the accuracy of your report.

What kind of emotions or feelings do you think you might experience? Anger? Overwhelmed? Tense? Uptight? Disoriented? Confused?

The Symptoms of ADD

Welcome to the world of the Attention Deficit Disorder. ADD is a condition that some children and adults experience which manifests itself through numerous symptoms which may include one or more of the following:

Hyperactivity -- They can't stay still. They are constantly moving and fidgeting. They are under chairs or tables or climbing over furniture.

Impulsiveness -- They move or change directions very quickly. They will be doing one thing and then suddenly start doing something else. They "act before they think!"

Distractibility -- They can't stay focused on one thought or task. They will be doing a task and the smallest noise interrupts them.

Lack of organization -- They cannot do the more complex tasks which require them to organize the larger task into a series of steps. Somebody has to tell or show them how to do each step.

Forgetfulness -- They forget instructions. They forget to do things or tasks they have been told to do. They will start to do something and forget what they were supposed to do.

Procrastination -- They have trouble starting and completing tasks or assignments. They are constantly putting off doing things. They can't seem to "get started."

Often these behaviors surface in school, frustrating both the teachers and the other students who are trying to learn. A student with ADD symptoms can be extremely disruptive in a classroom situation.

The current widespread, accepted treatment is medication. Although, for some it may be the only treatment, there are those parents and professionals who question the advisability of putting a child on drugs. Alternative treatments are being researched and one currently being investigated by this author is the use of Neuro-Linguistic Programming (NLP). NLP is sometimes described as a systemized set of procedures that allows the study of the processing of the mind and the resultant behaviors.

Research using NLP is based on the assumption that it is the child's internal experience or processing that is causing his difficult behaviors. Attempts have been made to determine what that internal

... is based on the assumption that it is the child's internal experience or processing that is causing his difficult behaviors.

experience is and to decide if it can be altered by various NLP techniques and processes, thereby bypassing the need for unwanted drugs. This part of the handbook is a report on that research.

The Subjective Experience of the Student With ADD Symptoms

First, let's look at what we have found as to the internal or subjective experience of a person with ADD symptoms. Some of the most important internal experiences that interact to influence the behavior of the student with ADD symptoms are:

- ♦ They perceive multiple internal images.
- ♦ These images are moving rapidly and sometimes mysteriously disappear.
- ♦ The images are often occurring simultaneously.
- ♦ There is a strong kinesthetic (body and/or emotional) response to the images.
- ♦ They can't control any of these internal experiences.

Some of the common responses of students with ADD symptoms to this internal chaos seem to be:

1. They either try to physically respond to everything in their internal pictures or they get frustrated and simply give up even trying. The final result is a person that is either hyperactive or apathetic and passive.

2. They feel they are losing control and will go to great lengths to control their internal experience and/or external world. The result is they spend an inordinate amount of time and energy trying to slow things down or organize their experience so that it is manageable.

3. They are often terrified at their lack of control and its consequences. Much of the time they have a feeling of being totally overwhelmed.

4. They suffer from fear of rejection and abandonment because they believe they are "different" or "weird." The feedback they receive from peers, parents and teachers often confirms these fears.

5. Their level of hyperactivity and the intensity of their emotional responses seems to be dependent on the standards significant others (such as family) use to judge and enforce their behavior. In other words, the stricter the parents and the more severe the punishment (or, to the degree the child perceives it is severe) the more hyperactive the child. Later on, they transfer this to teachers and peers as well.

6. They sometimes have tremendous suppressed anger or rage because of the perceived injustices in the way they have been treated by others. This shows up in hyperactivity, impulsiveness, and anti-social behavior.

> They sometimes have tremendous suppressed anger or rage because of the perceived injustices in the way they have been treated by others.

Why Do They Act That Way?

What about some of the typical behaviors or symptoms, if you will, that result from this condition? Can we explain how they manifest themselves in a student with ADD symptoms? Let's consider some of them.

Hyperactivity -- If you had multiple images flashing simultaneously in your head and you had a demand from a parent or teacher to "act right," or "behave", what do you think you would do? Many students with ADD symptoms respond by focusing on the internal pictures. And since they are typically very physical in nature, these fast-moving internal pictures generate an abundance of nervous energy. If they have suppressed rage, the fast moving pictures just add to the nervous energy. They act to relieve the body tension in the best way they know how -- **THEY MOVE THEIR BODIES**.

Impulsiveness -- This goes hand-in-hand with the hyperactive behavior. Because the students with ADD symptoms are trying to physically react to their internal experience as quickly as possible, they often respond by "doing it" before they consciously realize that the degree of their response isn't necessary. This phenomena is similar to a compulsive behavior in the rest of us. The students with ADD symptoms' compulsion simply move faster and change quicker. Again, suppressed rage only adds to the problem. This is true because the students with suppressed rage about the injustices that have been meted out to them are especially sensitive to how others treat them and they are sometimes very argumentative.

Distractibility -- Often the impulsive children described above are also labeled as distractable because they can't stay focused on one task. Their mind is often pulled off the task at hand by an idea that carries more kinesthetic (physical) weight to them. A prime example of this might be when they hear an unexpected noise in the classroom. They will immediately make an internal image of the possible cause and *have* to check it out by looking. Depending upon the nature of the distraction and the importance it carries internally for them, it may be extremely difficult for them to get re-focused.

Keep in mind that the students with ADD symptoms are experiencing a multitude of pictures moving quickly through their heads. Trying to keep up with 10 to 15 different images and trying to select appropriate responses to each would make most of us oversensitive to extra stimuli. The more angry and hyperactive they are, the worse it is.

Lack of Organization -- To be organized, a person must be able to visualize a total project and prioritize the specific steps needed to accomplish the finished project. This requires an ability to stabilize several internal pictures simultaneously. Students with ADD symptoms have trouble doing this because the pictures are moving too rapidly or are disappearing.

Most students with ADD symptoms have not learned yet how to take a general idea and break it down into its component parts while still retaining the general idea. Nor do they take many specific points and generalize the pattern they are observing. In a given moment, they are either general or specific. For example, if a typical student has a science project, he knows the overall purpose of the project, and the steps it will take to accomplish the project. He will be able to sequence the steps in order to efficiently accomplish the task. He will also be able to track the steps and the amount of time it will take to accomplish all of this. A student with ADD symptoms experiences great difficulty in doing this because he cannot stabilize the pictures.

Forgetfulness -- Remembering requires a clean, logical connection between the external cue which tells you *when it is time to do something* and the internal experience which tells you *what to do.* With all of the internal images students with ADD symptoms are experiencing, it is difficult for them to establish that clean connection. Also, the thing to be remembered must carry significant kinesthetic weight for them or it will be overwhelmed by all the other images and forgotten. Besides, if they have suppressed anger, forgetting to do things is a good way to do battle with authority figures.

> ...if they have suppressed anger, forgetting to do things is a good way to do battle.

Procrastination -- Often what is labeled procrastination is often inaction. The inaction results from an inability to make a definite and final decision that they can act on comfortably. This inaction is a natural result of being unable to process the rapidly changing, excess of information in their mind. Also, like in "forgetfulness", not doing things is a good way to fight.

Potential causes of the ADD Symptoms

What causes these behavioral symptoms? Why is it that some people have them temporarily and in others they persist over time? Is it possible that the symptoms are caused by different life events which need to be treated differently? My attempt to answer these questions follows.

The symptoms of Attention Deficit Disorder (ADD) are generated by the perception that the mind is out of control. This out of control mind can be initially caused by any one or any combination of the following:

1. High stress and anxiety.

2. Emotional trauma -- past or present.

3. Candida Albicans.

4. Attitude -- which can be boredom, or not being turned on to certain activities such as chores or schoolwork, or not knowing HOW to do the required tasks.

5. Communication gaps between the child and parents/teachers.

6. Physical reaction -- to large amounts of sugar or junk food or allergies (usually food).

For the most part, factors 1, 2, 3, and 6 are outside the scope of this publication. Factor 3 can be helped by going to a good health food store or to a physician who is knowledgeable about Candida. Books such as "The Yeast Syndrome" or "The Yeast Connection" can also help. Professionals such as Allergists, Dieticians, Physicians, and Psychologists are equipped to handle factors 1, 2, and 6. Factors 4 and 5 are covered in other parts of this book.

However, the perception or belief that the mind is out of control can be dealt with here and is covered in following sections.

> However, the perception or belief that the mind is out of control can be dealt with here and is covered in following sections.

A New Definition of ADD

I have found that many students are misdiagnosed with the label of ADD. The behavioral symptoms fit many persons (child and adult) who are highly stressed, suffer from trauma, are bored in school or work or who are acting out other behavioral problems. Many times teaching students how to learn in school, how to focus, how to organize, how to set priorities and/or how to have a better attitude in school causes the symptoms to go away.

Teaching parents, teachers, and students how to communicate better seems to help a great deal. I have also found that it is important to initially check for allergies, particularly food, and to check out the intake of sugar and/or junk food.

I have also found the ADD symptoms in individuals of all ages who have been infected with the yeast germ "Candida Albicans." But the most dominating feature that I have found is the inability to control

But the most dominating feature that I have found is the inability to control that mind **and the accompanying belief that their mind controls them or that they cannot control their mind.** The result of this causes major ramifications throughout the individual and creates far greater problems then previously thought.

that mind **and the accompanying belief that their mind controls them or that they cannot control their mind.** The result of this causes major ramifications throughout the individual and creates far greater problems then previously thought.   Because of this I've adjusted my definition of ADD.

My new definition is as follows: The symptoms of ADD seem to be caused by a loss of control of the processing of the mind which results in symptoms at **ALL** logical levels.* According to common knowledge, Attention Deficit Disorder is a set of behavioral symptoms. When we look at ADD

> My new definition is as follows: The symptoms of ADD seem to be caused by a loss of control of the processing of the mind which results in symptoms at **ALL** logical levels.

through the eyes of the logical levels we can get a sense of why the treatment of ADD is so difficult.

Environment Level--The person with ADD symptoms can do just fine in some environments and not in others. If they are by their self and without outside distractions, they can stay focused and accomplish tasks. Put them in a school or busy family setting, however, and they will start displaying many of the behavioral symptoms. In fact, in many instances, the environment is the triggering device for the behavioral symptoms.

Many of the treatments or interventions that are attempted are at this level. Students are seated away from other students so they will not be distracted by other activities going on in the classroom. Sometimes students are sent to special rooms that are especially quiet and have few auditory or visual distractions. Sometimes when they are at home they will be isolated in their rooms and told to study there and not be allowed TV or radio. Many with the

---

* See Appendix B: The Logical Levels of Experience

ADD symptoms will attempt to overly organize their environment in order to control the chaos they experience.

Behavior Level--This is the logical level that is most documented in all the literature. The behavioral symptoms of: impulsiveness, hyperactivity, forgetfulness, procrastination, distractibility, and lack of organization are clearly at this level. This level is also where most of the treatments or interventions are undertaken. Taking drugs is a behavior although the purpose for taking drugs is to deal with the next level--to be able to focus or control the mind. Many behavior modification techniques are attempted and are at this level. Learning how to organize their external environment is a behavior. The punishment and reward strategies are also at this level.

Capability Level--Most individuals with the symptoms of ADD feel as though their mind is out of control. Their internal experience is moving so fast and thoughts are appearing and disappearing and they feel unable to manage it. They cannot do the same things with their mind that other students seem to be able to do with ease. Learning and other academic tasks are very difficult for them because they cannot control and/or focus their mind. Drugs such as Ritalin are supposed to give them control over their mind and allow them to focus but the results are mixed.

> Most individuals with the symptoms of ADD feel as though their mind is out of control. Their internal experience is moving so fast and thoughts are appearing and disappearing and they feel unable to manage it.

Beliefs and Values Level--Most students with ADD symptoms believe that they cannot control their mind or that their mind controls them. They, therefore, are not responsible for what they do. They also develop limiting beliefs about the value of school and learning which guides their behaviors in school. They believe that school is dumb, boring, or at least a waste of time.

Identity Level--Many students who have had ADD symptoms a long time develop beliefs about their self which shows up in their self image or self esteem. They believe they are different or weird. Or, they will devalue themselves and think that they are worthless or that nobody likes them or accepts them. They also believe that they are totally discounted and not understood for who they REALLY are. Some rebel and fight back while others become apathetic and withdraw from society.

Spiritual/Greater Systems Level--Some students blame God for creating them differently. Some blame society or schools or family for not being able to help them. They feel as though they have been let down because nobody has been able to help them overcome this malady that they did not ask for. They feel like an outcast from society. They will sometimes strike out at society, families, schools, God or religions (and feel justified).

Obviously, simply treating the behavioral symptoms is not the complete intervention. Nor would it seem that drugs would be the complete answer. There are many issues and limiting beliefs which have to be ferreted out and dealt with in order to have a complete treatment.

Obviously, simply treating the behavioral symptoms is not the complete intervention. Nor would it seem that drugs would be the complete answer. There are many issues and limiting beliefs which have to be ferreted out and dealt with in order to have a complete treatment.

Techniques For Working With Students With ADD Symptoms

In parts of the following sections, I will refer to some Neuro-Linguistic Programming (NLP) change techniques such as the compulsion break, limiting belief change technique, logical level integration, or anchoring, etc. In writing this book, I had to decide if I wanted to write out NLP techniques for the non-

NLP trained readers but which are well known to practitioners of NLP or just suggest the technique to use by name and let them do it. I decided on the strategy to name some of the suggested intervention techniques and to not describe how to do it for the non-NLP trained readers. The primary reason is that the person doing the technique can do it far better if he or she has been trained and certified in NLP. For the non-NLP readers, I suggest you contact a certified practitioner of NLP to assist in some of these change processes. For assistance in locating one near you, please feel free to contact me at my office at SUCCESS SKILLS, Inc. in Oklahoma City, Oklahoma.

> For the non-NLP readers, I suggest you contact a certified practitioner of NLP to assist in some of these change processes. For assistance in locating one near you, please feel free to contact me at my office at SUCCESS SKILLS in Oklahoma City.

Teaching Students With ADD Symptoms How to Control Their Minds

The students not only have the inability to control their minds they believe that they can't do anything about it. Sometimes their mind terrifies them. This inability to control the mind drives all the symptoms listed previously. These persons will still need to learn the things listed above such as how to learn and have a proper attitude toward school, etc, but before they can learn these things they need to learn how to control their minds and to **BELIEVE** that they can.

My test for seeing if he can control his mind is to give him some simple tasks to do with his mind. One of these tasks is: Get an internal image of a <u>word he already knows how to spell</u> and hold the image steady while he is spelling it backwards (from right to left). I may gradually increase the length of the words until we have a fairly lengthy word (depending on their age). The person who cannot control their mind will not be able to hold the picture steady enough to do this. The word will fly away, fade away, jump around or simply disappear! And, he can't control the image. There are other people, by the way, who can't spell words or numbers backwards either. But, it is simply a matter of their learning how to do it and not because the word disappears or is out of control in their minds.

> Get an internal image of a <u>word he already knows how to spell</u> and hold the image steady while he is spelling it backwards (from right to left).

I like to start teaching them how to control their minds with simple non-school exercises. A successful and non-threatening way has been to use items such as pets, food, or some other physical item they like and **Do Not Connect To School.** For example, I might ask them to tell me what their favorite food is and then to describe what it looks like. When they can successfully do this (and I've never had one who was not able to), I assist them in becoming aware that they have an internal image of what it looks like. I then, while using NLP language pattern such as reframes and slight of mouth, start opening up the possibility that they can make their own adjustments in their internal images. I then start exploring sub-modalities with their internal image of pizza or ice cream or an apple (for example). I teach them to change the sub-modalities (size, distance, color, spatial location, brightness, etc) of their internal image.

Once they can do this with an apple, I get them to place a small word or letter on the apple. I sometimes start with only a letter, then two letters, then three, etc. I particularly work on having them make the apple with the letter or word on it bigger and/or closer. After awhile, when they can make a three to five letter word big and close, I ask them to hold a picture of the word (which they previously had trouble spelling backwards) steady while they tell me the last letter, then the letter right before it, then the next letter, and so on. All of a sudden, they realize that they have spelled the word backwards -- something they could **not** do only a short

> All of a sudden, they realize that they have spelled the word backwards -- something they could **not** do only a short while before.

while before. I have them continue to spell the word and other words backwards several more times because it gets easier and easier each time they do it. They are usually stunned and they don't know how to think about the new experience. So, I use this time as an opportunity to work on their beliefs about their capabilities and identity, what it means about controlling their own minds, and about school and learning (please refer to the section on how to change limiting beliefs).

> ...I use this time as an opportunity to work on their beliefs about their capabilities and identity, what it means about controlling their own mind, and about school and learning.

At this point, it becomes a process of building more instances of success so I give them longer words and numbers to make pictures of and spell backwards until they believe they can now control their images. At this point, I will either start teaching them how to learn and do the various academic tasks required of them to be successful in school or I will work on the specific symptoms of ADD and teach them how to control them. It usually depends on if the "ADD symptom" is getting in the way of learning how to be successful in school and/or at home.

Changing Limiting Beliefs of ADD

Sometimes I have to go for a limiting belief change before anything else will work. An example of this happened just recently. This young man, Jason, was brought to me from out of state by his family. The family had scheduled several days in Oklahoma City and I had cleared my calendar for them. The young man was 12 years old. According to his mother "He was hyperactive and impulsive as a child. At age 6, we had him tested at Children's Hospital for 3 days. They found him to be ADHD with all the symptoms. They medicated him with Ritalin and a wide range of other drugs through age 12. All were unsuccessful or caused severe side effects such as insomnia, anxiety, emotional problems, confusion, tics, etc. In the sixth grade he fell apart. He began showing signs of depression. He talked of death, was angry, frustrated, confused, and had low self esteem."

> "He was hyperactive and impulsive as a child. At age 6, we had him tested at Children's Hospital for 3 days. They found him to be ADHD with all the symptoms. They medicated him with Ritalin and a wide range of other drugs through age 12."

I had talked to the mother before we started about the possibility of working on Jason's limiting beliefs. This was primarily because of the shortness of time of their visit and the fact that I would not be available for follow-up. She had agreed upon this approach.

I started by asking Jason some questions about school and how he did in school just to build some rapport and to get to know how his mind worked. Shortly thereafter I had him spell several easy words which he already knew how to spell. After he could do that successfully, I had him attempt to spell a couple of them backwards to see if he could do it. The results were inconsistent and slow. Sometimes he could slowly spell them backwards and other times he could not. When I asked him to explain what happened to his pictures when he had trouble he said they disappeared -- just vanished. I would get him to try different sub-modalities such as size, distance, and brightness and the changes seemed to help him stabilize the pictures.

I switched to having him visualize an apple and to learn to move it around in his mind. He was more successful with the apple even when I started trying to get him to picture the word "apple" on the face of the apple. He could do this quite easily. When I started having him print longer words on the apple, he started getting frustrated. He started tearfully saying things, with frustration in his voice, like "I can't do this!" "This is not working." "Why do I have to do this?" and "I want to leave." We took a break. The statement "I can't do this!" is a limiting belief about his capability.

When we came back from the break, he was really into frustration and anger and he was tired. He wanted to quit. I decided immediately to shift to work on changing his belief. I asked him if he ever believed in the Easter Bunny or Santa Claus. He had. I then asked him if he still believed in them. He did not. I asked him to describe what had happened and asked him to consider how it was possible that he once believed in something and now did not. He described how some friends had made some comments that made him wonder about Santa Claus, then he had thought about how impossible it was for Santa Claus to travel that far that fast, and then he had caught his parents putting presents under the tree.

> I ... asked him to consider how it was possible that he once believed in something and now did not.

I told him that those were the natural steps to changing a belief: first, you would start to doubt it because you would experience some counter examples; second, the evidence would build up in support of the disbelief; and then, third, it would become an old belief that you no longer believed. Then you are open to replace it with a new belief which serves you better. I gave him several other examples of times in which he had believed something and had gone through the same process (e.g., Easter Bunny, tooth fairy, couldn't walk or ride bike but then he learned how, etc).

We are constantly adopting new beliefs about ourselves and life and using them until they no longer serve us and then discarding them and adopting newer beliefs which are more relevant," I said. "It is a natural process of growing. One of your limiting beliefs right now is that your brain controls you instead of you controlling your brain. Therefore, when you get bored or frustrated, you act out inappropriately -- and you believe you don't have any choices." "Do you know the major difference between yourself and me?" I asked. "You believe that your mind controls you and I believe that I can use my mind to accomplish anything I want in the world."

> "We are constantly adopting new beliefs about ourselves and life and using them until they no longer serve us and then discarding them and adopting newer beliefs which are more relevant."

> "Do you know the major difference between yourself and me?" I asked. "You believe that your mind controls you and I believe that I can use my mind to accomplish anything I want in the world."

Jason went into several extreme counter examples like throwing a football to the moon, staying alive if somebody shot me in the head, and so on... I agreed with him that I probably couldn't do those things but that there were some more simple things where his mind was getting him in trouble and that my mind did not get me into trouble.

"For example," I said "when you get bored in school, you disrupt the class by making noise, moving about, or by leaving the classroom. When I am bored, I figure out a way to entertain myself with my mind. I remember when I first learned to do that," I continued. "I was in the 5th grade and I was having to sit through long and boring church services and not get in trouble. I remembered figuring out that I could sit still while looking at the preacher and daydream in my mind of something I had rather be doing or make up a movie of something interesting. My mother and her friends thought I was very attentive to the sermon. I stayed out of trouble and didn't get bored." "Do you know that I still use that strategy to this day if I have to do something boring -- like work out at the spa or mow the lawn?" I added.

Jason then came up with some more counter examples like, "You can't make a million dollars suddenly appear" or "You can't heal yourself if you are sick." I then proceeded to share stories with him of how I had changed a limiting belief about money being evil to a more useful belief which would support my career in helping others. The new belief had dramatically affected my income. Also, I related some stories about how we were able to assist people with allergies, asthma, cancer, etc. by eliciting their limiting beliefs about their health and assisting them in changing the limiting beliefs to beliefs which would empower their own natural healing. I then showed Jason a picture on my wall of myself walking on fire. I told him that walking on fire was an example of how the mind was so powerful in controlling the body. He was surprised and tried to deny it -- but the photo clearly shows flames in the coals.

Jason started thinking about some possibilities and I started clearing some space so I could physically walk him through a belief change process. As Jason went through the process, you could see a physical change in him. His eyes and focus become clearer and more steady. He became totally attentive to what I was doing and the possibilities. He had changed his old belief of "My mind controls me!" to "I can use my mind to accomplish anything I want!"

> He had changed his old belief of "My mind controls me!" to
> "I can use my mind to accomplish anything I want!"

After we finished, I future paced the new belief into several times in his life where I knew he had previously had trouble, such as when he became bored or angry in school. "Awesome!" was his response. "I can do this!" was another. He said, "This is just like running a movie in my mind and I'm the director."

We then went back to doing some of the spelling words in his mind where he previously could not spell them backwards. He could now spell them backwards easily. We expanded the length of the words. He could still do it. He asked me, "what is the longest word you have ever spelled backwards?" I replied, **"Super-cali-fragi-listic-expi-ali-docious."** Luckily he didn't have me prove it since it had been a long time since I had done it.

We broke for lunch and I instructed him and his mother to play the game of noticing billboards and street signs and spelling them backwards to each other. When they came back from lunch they were happily and easily spelling all sorts of words and numbers backwards. We continued to work on other learning strategies as examples that he could learn how to use his mind to be successful in whatever he wanted.

I also pointed out to him that when he tried to learn something and it was hard that it just meant that he needed to learn another way or that he needed to break it down into smaller tasks. I told him that in those instances all he had to do was "back off for a moment and remember that he could use his mind to accomplish anything." I also reminded him about the time when he was very young and learning to walk and that "that little Jason didn't get frustrated and quit when he fell down then -- and aren't you glad now that little Jason didn't give up back then and that he persisted and kept trying?"

Logical Level Integration

I then physically walked Jason through the Logical Level Alignment Process which helps him integrate the new belief at all levels. To do this, I asked Jason the following questions as he stood in the various levels:

ENVIRONMENT -- "Where, when, and with whom will you use the new belief 'I can use my mind to accomplish anything I want!?' "
Jason -- "At school, at home, with my teachers, friends, and family."

BEHAVIOR -- "What will you do in those places and with those people to support your new belief 'I can use my mind to accomplish anything I want!?' What actions or behaviors will you do?"
Jason --"At school when I get bored or angry, I will stop and run a different movie in my mind which will let me relax. Also, when I can't do something, instead of getting angry, I will use my mind to figure out a different way to do it. I will also use your learning strategies so I won't get frustrated in school and with my teachers and mom. I will be calmer and will have more friends because I won't have to try to get attention anymore to get people to like me."

CAPABILITY -- "How will you accomplish those behaviors with your mind? Since you have your new belief 'I can use my mind to accomplish anything I want!' What will you do with your mind to do those actions at home and at school?"
Jason -- "By learning to run different movies in my mind to calm me down and to help me get what I want. I can also learn how to think better."

BELIEFS/VALUES -- "What new and different beliefs and values will you have now that you have the new belief 'I can use my mind to accomplish anything

I want!' What new things would a person with this belief focus on and value?"
Jason --"Value learning, doing well in school, friends, challenges."

IDENTITY -- "What kind of person would have these values and beliefs, these capabilities and do these behaviors? What kind of attributes would this kind of person have?"

Jason -- "Intelligence, patience, doing things well, and an 'I can do it attitude', accomplishing things."

The next day when Jason and his mother returned, he was calm and happy. As we warmed up his mind, he could easily and effectively spell words such as hypothermia and Saskatchewan frontwards and backwards. He took great pride in the fact that he was able to spell words backwards faster than his mother.

The ADD Dance

Sometimes the hyperactivity and other symptoms are caused by suppressed anger or by rage. Usually this comes from the long history they have had of being mistreated and labeled as weird or different or that "something is wrong with them." Their perception that they would act better if they could -- but they can't -- coupled with the fact that nobody seems to be able to help them, fuels the rage because of the total unfairness of the situation.

> Their perception that they would act better if they could -- but they can't -- coupled with the fact that nobody seems to be able to help them, fuels the rage because of the total unfairness of the situation.

The best remedies I have found for this type of rage is to lead them through a Re-imprint Process or to install a strategy. Probably the easiest intervention to use for suppressed rage (for a younger child, anyway) is to install a strategy for helping them interrupt the anger. I have used the following strategy for not only suppressed anger or rage but the ADD symptoms of impulsiveness, procrastination, hyperactivity and distractibility.

The strategy I have designed for anger and/or other ADD symptoms is called **The ADD Dance** which goes as follows:

A. On four pieces of paper write out the following:
   1. Situations or contexts where they lose control and get angry or exhibit the ADD symptom.
   2. First signal that they are BEGINNING to get angry or exhibit the symptom.
   3. A state of calmness and/or control and/or peace and/or the internal state which is wanted in place of the ADD symptom.
   4. A state of feeling good about self and/or confidence.

Place the four pieces of paper on the floor in a straight line with about 1-2 feet between each piece of paper.

B. At this time, establish the internal states for pieces of paper 2 - 4. **START WITH #3.** Have the person remember a time when he was completely calm and in control of himself. Have him think of a body position and/or gesture and/or sound that symbolizes that state. Jason, the young man previously mentioned, chose a standing lotus position for his. Then have him get into the internal state **with the body position/gesture/sound WHILE STANDING ON THE PIECE OF PAPER.** This connects the internal state to the paper.

Repeat the process for paper #4. Be sure he gets into the body position/gesture/sound. (Jason chose a pumping of the fist in the air while saying out loud, "All right!") Then repeat the process for paper #2. Be sure to let him BARELY get into the angry or ADD state. He should access only the VERY FIRST SIGNAL in his mind or body that lets him know that he is about to get angry -- then interrupt him and have him step off of the paper while you distract him. (Jason's signal was a tightening in his chest and the sensation that his chest was expanding). His mother imaged a red liquid rising in her body and head, like in a thermometer, with an accompanying spreading warmth.

C. Now have him think of a time or context where he could or did get angry and step onto paper #1. **As soon as he STARTS** to get into the situation, have him step onto paper #2 and do the body position/ gesture/sound. **AS SOON as he STARTS** to feel the anger or ADD symptom, have him step onto paper #3 and do the body position/gesture/sound. Have him stay there long enough to really get into the calmness. Then have him step onto paper #4 and really get into feeling good about himself. Let him stay here for a longer period of time while duplicating the body position/gesture/ sound for feeling good and confident.

D. Repeat step C for other times and contexts where he could become angry in the future. Have him become aware that as he tries this in more contexts, he will have to move from paper to paper faster because the brain is streamlining the strategy. In fact, have him make it a dance which incorporates the different body positions/gestures/sounds into a fluid dance which easily flows from one state to the next. You can even get him to put it to music of his choice. After a while, when you present him with a potential situation that USED to make him mad, he will have trouble getting into the anger.

> ...have him make it a dance which incorporates the different body positions/gestures/sounds into a fluid dance which easily flows from one state to the next.

This **ADD Dance** is meant to be an interruption of their normal way of losing control. It does not deal with the issues which generate the suppressed anger or the ADD symptom. The pent up anger or rage has probably built up over the years from mistreatment and traumatic situations and these issues need to be dealt with completely. The ADD Dance, however, will help gain access to their mind.

After using the ADD Dance, I find I can deal with the other ADD symptoms by teaching them how to use their mind the way the rest of us do. Some of these techniques follow.

The ADD Symptom of Distractibility

Because of the fact that students with ADD symptoms are looking at multiple pictures that are unstable or moving very rapidly, it is difficult for them to stay focused on one task. They, therefore, come across as being distracted. They never think about the fact that they don't have to continue to look at all the pictures at the same time.

To teach them a different way, I have them get into a distracted mode in which they have the multiple pictures. I then instruct them to imagine themselves reaching up and grabbing one of the pictures and "pulling it down close and making it very big -- just as they did the picture of the apple or the words they spelled backwards!" When they do this they typically have a startled response because all the other pictures go away (are blocked out) and they can concentrate on the one big and close picture. I then start to talk to them about how the skill of focus is in selecting one of the many pictures and pulling it close and making it bigger and dealing with it until they are through. Then, putting it back in place and grabbing another and pulling it close and making it bigger.

Once the students have learned and believe that it is possible for them to control their minds and internal experience, the other symptoms of ADD tend to go away fairly rapidly.

The most amazing thing about this is that their unconscious mind seems to get the idea after only a few demonstrations and will automatically do it later on. It's as though their minds have been looking for a solution, and as soon as one is offered that works, it is latched on to it very quickly. Once the students have learned and believe that it is possible for them to control their minds and internal experience, the other symptoms of ADD tend to go away fairly rapidly.

The ADD Symptom of Hyperactivity

By this time many of the signs of hyperactivity have started to go away. Since the hyperactivity was caused by the multiple pictures and their instability and speed AND by the fear of losing control of the mind, the ability to bring one picture close and big and concentrate on it causes them to calm down. This will be particularly true if you have dealt with any suppressed rage they have had. The most common remarks of the student or their parent who is observing is, "They have never been like this before!" or "They have never been able to do this before!" or "They have never been this focused for this long!" The instruction to them regarding being hyperactive

Since the hyperactivity was caused by the multiple pictures and their instability and speed AND by the fear of losing control of the mind, the ability to bring one picture close and big and concentrate on it causes them to calm down.

is, "When you feel yourself losing control or becoming hyper, focus on one thing at a time by bringing it close and big." I usually anchor or stabilize this more relaxed, focused state and, later on, turn the anchor over to them.

The ADD Symptom of Impulsiveness

I have found that the impulsiveness can be dealt with in four ways; with the compulsion break in specific situations, with a belief change usually around their vulnerability, with a strategy intervention in which we install a strategy for pausing and thinking things out (the ADD Dance), and by dealing with suppressed anger as I referred to earlier (the anger can sometimes cause the impulsiveness -- they are like a time bomb).

Many students with ADD symptoms have a compulsion to physically look at any new external input, particularly if it is auditory. If I deem it is the typical compulsion level type response, then I will lead them through a series of compulsion breaks on the specific ones that give them the most trouble. While I am doing this, I am instructing their unconscious mind to generalize the compulsion break.

Other students with ADD symptoms, especially the hyperactive ones, have a belief about themselves that makes them very sensitive to their outside world. They feel very vulnerable because they have been so different. They usually have been severely admonished, criticized, and ridiculed. They sometimes are almost paranoid and are overly sensitive or alert to what is going on around them. To some, this sensitivity is a survival skill. In these types of cases, I elicit their limiting belief and change it.

Other students with ADD symptoms, especially the hyperactive ones, have a belief about themselves that makes them very sensitive to their outside world. They feel very vulnerable because they have been so different.

The most common treatment I use for impulsiveness is at the strategy level. I find that most students with ADD symptoms have simply programmed their minds and bodies to react in an impulsive fashion. They have done this for good reason but now the reason is no longer there. Simply designing and installing an appropriate decision-making strategy about thinking before they act seems to work well. Or, if you can find a context in which they already react normally, recontextualizing the strategy works very quickly.

The ADD Symptom of Forgetfulness

I work on forgetfulness on three levels; how to communicate for the parent and teacher, how to process auditory instructions for the students with ADD symptoms, and how to utilize a strategy for remembering when to do things.

Since most students with ADD symptoms have a tight V-K synthesia, auditory input is not processed unless they overlap the words into Visual or Kinesthetic experience. By now, this is a fairly easy skill to teach them. Teaching parents and teachers to use visual language and/or teaching them how to make sure that the student with ADD symptoms has visually processed their instructions seems to be important to the communication process. Many parents and teachers assume that just because they told them to do something means they processed it. This is not so! The student with ADD symptoms has to overlap the instructions into the visual or kinesthetic field or the parent or teacher has to visually communicate or demonstrate it.

> Many parents or teachers assume that just because they told them to do something means they processed it. This is not so!

Many people including students with ADD symptoms can benefit from a strategy for remembering to do things when they want to do them. Simply teaching them to design and install the internal experience of what they want to remember to do and then anchoring it to a reliable external cue works wonders (see the section on how to remember to do things).

The ADD Symptom of Lack of Organization

The most common intervention I use on the lack of organization is to teach them the skill of "chunking down." Because of the way their mind has worked in the past, they never thought it possible to take a general concept or idea and hold it steady in their mind while they broke it down into steps or parts. Since the primary skill of organization is to take complex tasks and break them down into smaller tasks or steps and prioritize them, the students with ADD symptoms have never before learned this basic skill. Now that they know how to stabilize ideas in their mind, this skill is a natural next step to learn.

The ADD Symptom of Procrastination

Much of procrastination is about decision-making. Decision-making is about gathering high quality information, setting priorities, and setting realistic deadlines. Now that their internal world is more stable, they can now learn these skills which were foreign to them before now.

Some Tips for Parents and Teachers

Research using NLP is still ongoing regarding precise ways to teach the students with ADD symptoms how to manage their minds or internal experience. There are, however, some simple things that the parent or teacher can do to help alleviate the situation or at least not make it worse.

1. Look for the positive intention in the students with ADD symptoms. They are doing the very best they know how. **Accept and appreciate them as very unique persons who are just a simple step or two away from being geniuses.** They are just having a hard time fitting in with the system -- both educational and family. The biggest obstacle to overcome for a student with ADD symptoms is that they are labeled "stupid, weird, or different" as though something is wrong with them. Consistently looking for positive intention and accepting and appreciating them as unique persons with value will go a long way in helping them overcome this belief.

Look for the positive intention in the students with ADD symptoms. They are doing the very best they know how. **Accept and appreciate them as very unique persons who are just a simple step or two away from being geniuses.** They are just having a hard time fitting in with the system -- both educational and family.

2. Being verbal or auditory is the least important communication channel to the students with ADD symptoms. They live in the world of internal images and the emotional and physical response to those images. Words are very slow and difficult to process for them. If you have to give instructions to a student with ADD symptoms, have him overlap the words into internal action pictures and have him FEEL his body doing it. For example, if you want him to carry out the trash and then do his homework, have him SEE and FEEL himself taking out the trash and then sitting down and opening his school book.

3. In school, make sure they visually learn as is outlined in other sections of this handbook AND make sure they do not fall into auditory learning strategies. They need to make pictures of such academic tasks as learning spelling words, the meaning of vocabulary words, and their math facts. In fact, make sure they visualize any data they are required to memorize. Also, when they read they should overlap the words into internal images of the meaning of the reading material. Most of the visual learning strategies are covered in the first part of this book. They work well with the students with ADD symptoms who can now stabilize their images.

Summary

Most students with ADD symptoms are very intelligent. In fact, the very qualities of their internal experiences that are causing them the most trouble are qualities often found in creative problem-solvers.

Most students with ADD symptoms are very intelligent. In fact, the very qualities of their internal experiences that are causing them the most trouble are qualities often found in creative problem-solvers. Most children and adults who experience these same multiple pictures in their minds have an ability to control their internal experience so that it does not translate into the behavioral symptoms that cause problems. By contrast, **the child or adult with ADD symptoms is controlled by his internal experience**. The obvious solution is to teach the students with ADD symptoms how to control their internal experience so they can be more effective. There are ways to do this utilizing various interventions and processes of NLP. These processes include teaching the students with ADD symptoms how to control the number and speed of the internal images.

This approach seems to work quite easily and quickly. Most of us, as well as the students with ADD symptoms, never think of doing things differently with our minds because most of the internal processing is out of conscious awareness. We don't realize there may be a better way, so we keep doing what we know to do. In most cases, all that is needed is some guidance in how to do it differently AND in a way that works really well. The beauty

Most of us, as well as the students with ADD symptoms, never think of doing things differently with our minds because most of the internal processing is out of conscious awareness. We don't realize there may be a better way, so we keep doing what we know to do.

of Neuro-Linguistic Programming (NLP) is that it offers the very set of skills which will allow us to interface with the students with ADD symptoms at that level. Hopefully, this publication will stimulate NLP research into even better ways to help these much maligned individuals.

APPENDIX A

WHAT IS "NLP" OR NEURO-LINGUISTIC PROGRAMMING?

Neuro-Linguistic Programming (NLP) is the process of modeling conscious and unconscious subjective experience of human systems. These systems may be inside one human, or between two humans, or among many humans. NLP modeling is the art of revealing the underlying structure of the subjective experience and codifying it in such a way that it is learnable by others. The results are NLP models of subjective experience.

These NLP models sometimes manifest themselves in the form of techniques for quickly and effectively altering patterns of behavior, capability, thought, and belief. Mastery of NLP provides you with specific, learnable skills and techniques which can help you improve your level of performance, resolve sources of tension, overcome limitations, and achieve higher levels of confidence in virtually any area of your life.

NLP can be very effectively used in personal situations ranging from smoking, weight, phobias and anxiety attacks, drug abuse, sexual abuse (to name just a few) to relationship problems.

It has also been successfully applied in a wide number of professions such as business, education, mental health, medicine, sports, law, and communication.

APPENDIX B

THE LOGICAL LEVELS OF EXPERIENCE

Too many times we find ourselves engaged in repetitive communication or personal change attempts in which we are trying to solve a problem. One reason our attempts do not work is because we keep trying to solve the problem at the same logical level at which it was created. Most of the time the real solution lies at a higher logical level. The following gives you a guideline to help pin-point the appropriate level at which we can be the most effective in personal communication or personal change.

Logical Levels

Spiritual/Greater System -- Attempts at this level affects our experience of being a part of a much vaster system. Answer to the question of WHO ELSE DOES THIS BEHAVIOR SERVE? Or, WHAT IS THE GREATER PURPOSE OR VISION?

Identity -- Attempts at this level affects self-image and overall purpose. Answers the question of WHO AM I?

Beliefs and Values -- Attempts at this level affects the motivation and permission by affecting the reasons that we do it. Answers the question of WHY DO I DO IT?

Capabilities -- Attempts at this level affects behavioral actions through a mental map, skill or strategy. Answers the question of HOW DO I DO IT?

Behavior -- Attempts at this level affects specific actions or behaviors taken within the environment. Answers the question of WHAT DO I DO?

Environment -- Attempts to change at this level affects the external constraints a person has to live within and react to. This level answers the questions of WHERE and/or WHEN and/or WITH WH0M DO I DO IT?

For more information on the Logical Levels, please refer to Gregory Bateson's "Steps to an Ecology of Mind" and/or Robert Dilts' "Beliefs--Pathway to Health and Well-Being" or his newest book "Visionary Leadership Skills." These are all listed in the Bibliography.

BIBLIOGRAPHY

Anderson, Jill. *Thinking, Changing, Rearranging: Improving Self-Esteem in Young People.* Portland, OR: Metamorphous Press, 1981.

Armstrong, Thomas. *In Their Own Way.* Los Angeles, CA: J.P. Tarcher, Inc., 1987.

Bain, L. . *A Parents Guide to Attention Deficit Disorders*, New York: Dell, 1991.

Bateson, Gregory. *Steps to an Ecology of Mind.* New York: Harper & Row, 1972.

Beecher, Henry K. *The Measurement of Subjective Response.* New York: Oxford University Press, 1959.

Bell, Nanci. *Visualizing & Verbalizing.* Paso Robles, CA: Academy of Reading Publications, 1986.

Blackerby, Don A. Crisis in Education: The Wasting of Our Children, Lakewood, CO, Cahill Mountain Press, *Anchor Point Journal,* August, 1989.

Blackerby, Don A. Brain Tuneup, Lakewood, CO, Cahill Mountain Press, *Anchor Point Journal*, September, 1994

Blackerby, Don A. Attention Deficit Disorder (ADD)--An NLP Perspective, Lakewood, CO, Cahill Mountain Press, *Anchor Point Journal,* December, 1994.

Blackerby, Don A. *Attention Deficit Disorder (ADD)--NLP Interventions That Work,* Salt Lake City, UT, Anchor Point Journal, Anchor Point Associates, October, 1995

Carbo, Marie; Dunn, Rita; and Dunn Kenneth. *Teaching Students to Read Through Their Individual Learning Styles.* Englewood Cliff, New Jersey: Prentice Hall, 1986.

Comings, D.E. *Tourette Syndrome and Human Behavior.* California: Hope Press, 1990.

Cowart, V.S. "The ritalin controversy: what's made this drug's opponents hyperactive?" *Journal of the American Medical Association*, 259, 2521-2523. 1988.

Cummings, Dr. Carol. *Teaching Makes a Difference.* Edmond, Washington: Teaching, Inc., 1980.

Dilts, Robert, *Changing Beliefs*, Meta Publications, 1990.

Dilts, Robert, *Visionary Leadership Skills*,Meta Publications, 1996

Dilts, Robert, Hallbom, Tim, and Smith, Suzi, *Beliefs: Pathways to health and Well-Being*, Metamorphous Press, 1990.

Dilts, Robert, and Epstein, Todd, *Dynamic Learning*. Capitola, CA, Meta Publications, 1995

Dardig, J.C. and Heward, W.L. *Sign Here: A Contracting Book for Children and Their Parents.* Bridgewater, New Jersey: F. Fournies & Associates, 1981.

Fenker, R. and Mullins, R. *Stop Studying and Start Learning.* Fort Worth. Texas: Tangram Press, 1982.

Ferguson, Marilyn. *Aquarian Conspiracy.* Los Angeles, California: J.P. Tarcher, 1980.

Gauthier, M. "Stimulant medications in adults with attention deficit disorder". *Canadian Journal of Psychiatry*, 439 (29), 435-440, 1984.

Goldstein, S. And Goldstein, M. *Managing Attention Disorders in Children.* New York: John Wiley and Sons, 1990.

Golin, M., Bricklin, M. Diamond, D. And the Rodale Center for Executive Development. *Secrets of Executive Success.* Emmaus, PA: Rodale Press, 1991.

Goodlad, John. *A Place Called School.* New York: McGraw-Hill, 1984.

Grinder, M. *Righting the Educational Conveyor Belt.* Portland, OR., Metamorphous Press, 1990.

Hartmann, T., Focus your Energy: Hunting for Success In Business With ADD. New York: 1994

Holmes, Thomas and Rahe. "The Social Readjustment Rating Scale." *Journal of Psychosomatic Research,* 11, 1967.

Ingersoll, B. *Your Hyperactive Child: A Parent's Guide to Coping with attention Deficit Disorder.* New York: Doubleday. 1988

Jacobson, S., *Meta-Cation, Vols I, II, and III.* Capitola, CA: Meta Publications, 1983, 1986, 1987.

Johnson, David; Holubec, Roger; and Johnson; Edythe. *Cooperation in the Classroom.* Edina, MN: Interaction Book Company., 1988.

Kelly, K., Ramundo, P. *You Mean I'm Not Lazy, Stupid or Crazy?!,* Cincinnati, OH, 1993.

Lapp, D. *Don't Forget: Easy Exercises for a Better Memory at Any Age.* New York: McGraw-Hill, 1987.

Lee, Scout. *The Excellence Principle.* Portland, OR: Metamorphous Press, 1989.

Levine, M.D. *Developmental Variation and Learning Disorders.* Cambridge, MA: Educators Publishing Service, Inc., 1987.

Levine, M.D. *Keeping Ahead in School.* Cambridge, MA: Educators Publishing Service, Inc. 1990.

Lewis, Byron and Pucelik, Frank. *Magic Demystified.* Portland, OR: Metamorphous Press, 1982.

Lloyd, Linda. *Classroom Magic.* Portland, OR:Metamorphous Press, 1982.

Lorayne H. and Lucas, J. *The Memory Book.* NewYork: Dorset Press, 1974.

McCarthy, Bernice. *4MAT.* Barrington, IL: Excel. Inc., 1981.

Miller, Patrick. *Nonverbal Communication.* Washington, D.C.: National Education Association, 1981.

Naisbitt, John. *Megatrends.* New York: Warner Books, 1984.

O'Connor, Joseph, Seymour, J., *Introducing Neuro-Linguistic Programming.* Cornwall, England, Aquarian Press, 1990.

O'Connor, Joseph. *Not Pulling Strings.* Portland, OR: Metamorphous Press, 1989.

Van Nagel, C., Reese, E., Reese, M., Siudzinski, R., *Megateaching and Learning.* Indian Rocks Beach, FL: Southern Institute Press, 1985.

Satir, V. *Making Conta~~ct~~* ~~...~~ Celestial Arts, 1976.

Scheiber, B. and Talpers, J. *Unlocking Potential: College and Other Choices for Learning Disabled People -- A Step by Step Guide.* Baltimore, MD: Adler and Adler, 1987.

Silver, L.B. *Attention-Deficit Hyperactivity Disorder: A Clinical Guide to Diagnosis and Treatment.* Washington, DC: American Psychiatric Press, Inc, 1991.

Tannen, D. *You Just Don't Understand.* New York: William Morrow and Company, 1990.

Turecki, S. *The Difficult Child.* New York: Bantam, 1985.

Weiss, L. *Attention Deficit Disorder in Adults: Practical Help for Sufferers and Their Spouses.* Dallas, TX: Taylor Publishing., 1992.

Wender, P.H. *The Hyperactive Child, Adolescent, and Adult: Attention Deficit Disorder Through the Lifespan.* New York: Oxford University Press, 1987.

Winston, S. *Getting Organized.* New York: Warner Books, 1978.

Wolkenberg, F. . "Out of a darkness". *New York Times Magazine,* pp. 62, 66, 70, 82-83, October 11, 1987.